# Former Synagogues of the United States

# Former Synagogues of the United States

## Looking at Buildings That Once Housed Synagogues, Schools, and Other Jewish Institutions

ELLEN LEVITT

RESOURCE *Publications* · Eugene, Oregon

FORMER SYNAGOGUES OF THE UNITED STATES
Looking at Buildings That Once Housed Synagogues, Schools, and Other Jewish Institutions



Resource Publications
An Imprint of Wipf and Stock Publishers
199 W. 8th Ave., Suite 3
Eugene, OR 97401

www.wipfandstock.com

PAPERBACK ISBN: 978-1-6667-7347-7
HARDCOVER ISBN: 978-1-6667-7348-4
EBOOK ISBN: 978-1-6667-7349-1

VERSION NUMBER 02/10/26

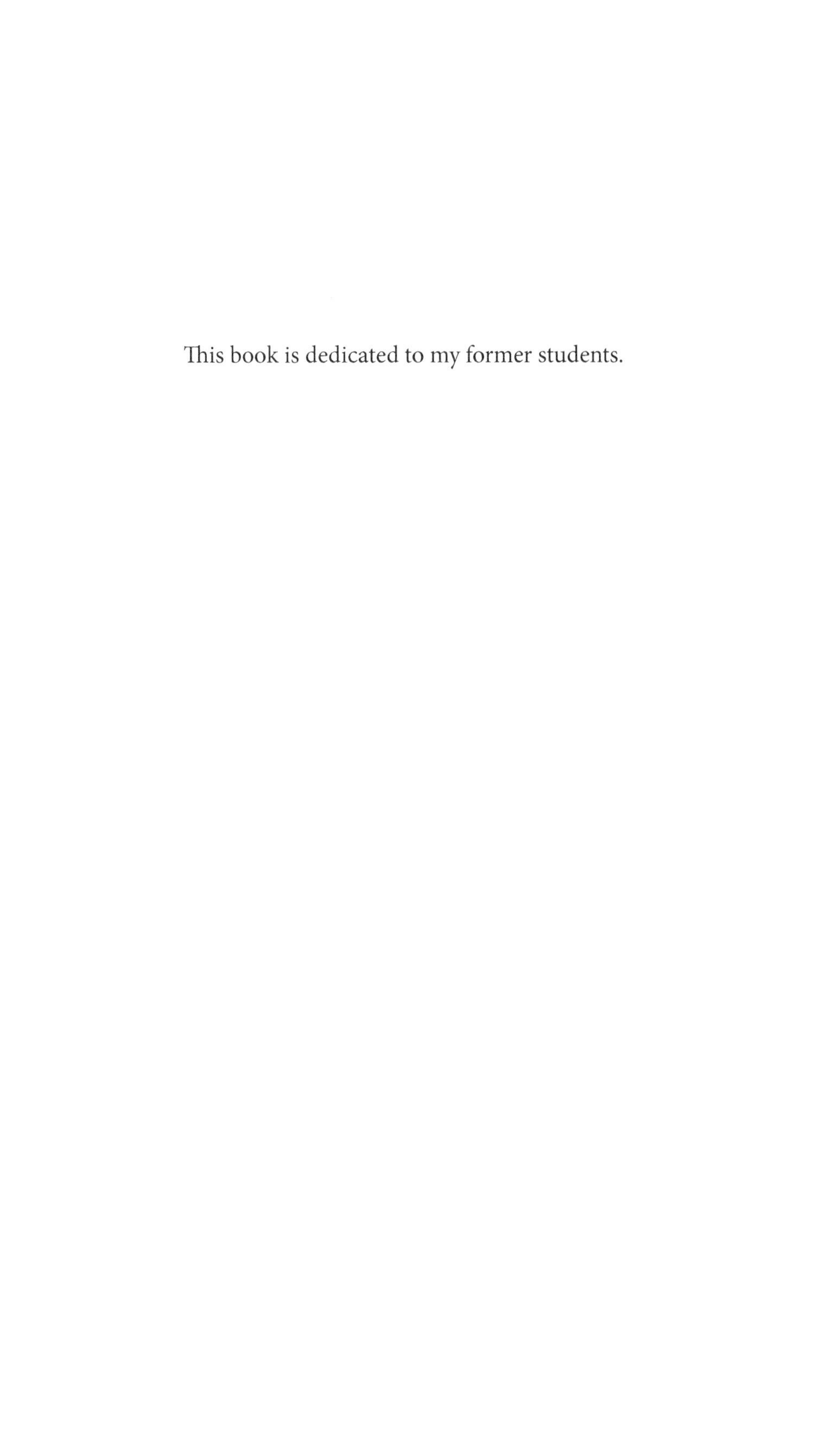

This book is dedicated to my former students.

# Contents

# Introduction

In June 2022, my family and I vacationed in San Francisco. While there we visited my relatives, took cable car rides, strolled through the De Young Museum of Art, and engaged in other typical tourist activities. But one less typical thing we did was stop by a house at 3535 19th Street in the Mission District.

I drove our rental car to this building and snapped several cell phone photographs. I looked carefully at the pretty details of this building, including the Jewish stars on the exterior, as well as on several windows and the front gate. I knew in advance that this building, which is now an apartment building, was once a synagogue known as Temple B'nai David. This building ceased to function as a synagogue in 1978, and was turned into private housing. Yet it still retains a good deal of recognizable Judaica on its exterior.

The 19th Street building is well maintained and has a quiet charm. Contrast this with an apartment building at 165 Henry Street in Manhattan's Lower East Side. I've walked by this building several times since 2010, and it often seems a bit disheveled, with overflowing garbage cans, clothes hanging off of window guards, and smatterings of graffitti. Look carefully to notice that the exterior of this building has several pieces of Judaica as well. There are Jewish stars set in the brick near the roofline, as well as a decorative motif reminiscent of the Ten Commandments. Decades ago this was a Jewish school with a synagogue on the premises, and was known as the Rabbi Jacob Joseph School. In fact, there is a concrete sign near the front entrance that states this.

Yet another apartment building I have seen, in Kingston, New York, was also built as a synagogue. The 19th century building at 50 Abeel Street was converted into housing units. And while this building does not exhibit overt Judaica, it features a split-in-half Ten Commandments decalogue with Roman numerals. The first time I saw this building was in 2019, when I drove within the Hudson Valley city with my family; my older daughter attended college at nearby SUNY New Paltz, and we were in search of a restaurant. We passed this particular brick building, and I slowed the car, gazed at #50, and had an inkling that it may have been a synagogue at some point. Two years later, my hunch was confirmed by research.

I have documented former synagogues in several cities, suburbs and small towns around the United States. Many have been turned into houses of worship for other religions, and now serve as churches, mosques or sites for Asian faiths. Other former synagogues have been repurposed as medical centers, schools, an art gallery, museums, event spaces, a hotel, and so on. I have seen other former synagogues that were renovated into housing, including one in New Orleans, a brick edifice from the 1860s that was built as Shaare Tefillah.

These might seem like curiosities to most people, but since the late 1980s, when I first became aware of a former Brooklyn synagogue that had become a church, I have been fascinated by these sites. They interest me for various reasons: because I am Jewish, and taught history on the high school level for many years, and have strong interests in architecture, stained glass windows, and in genealogy. Even as a child, I was intrigued by buildings that had been changed into Something Else: a former movie theater that became a church, a former bank that became a store, an old bowling alley that became a store; and so on.

But there is more to this than just general curiosity, on my part. I have wondered why communities would invest so much money, time and emotion into buildings, and then those communities would vacate the buildings, and other groups come in later on. Why did two Jewish congregations build huge, ornate synagogues on High Street in Newark, then leave them and build spiritual homes in suburbia? Why did Jewish families build a large synagogue in downtown Syracuse and then abandon it? Why was a small synagogue in Baltimore built and then turned into a church?

There are general trends, and there are individual stories. The fortunes of cities and towns wax and wane. Religious groups expand and contract, merge with one another, move to other locales. Therefore, there are several reasons why congregations will leave synagogue buildings. Occasionally there are happy and fortuitous reasons, but often they are melancholy, bittersweet, driven by fear or sadness and unfortunate financial realities.

In the United States these synagogue closings have been more or less voluntary. Unlike the many Central and Eastern European synagogues that closed due to the Holocaust and events leading up to it, such as Kristallnacht, and unlike the pogroms and the Farhud that shuttered synagogues in Middle Eastern and North African communities, the American synagogues that closed have done so not due to rabid persecution and expulsion, but more often due to socio-economic reasons, shifting populations, changing customs, and more. Some did suffer from antisemitic acts, or theft and vandalism, even arson; and some were deteriorating physically, but the American Jewish communities were not facing the extremely harsh conditions found on other continents.

Some synagogues closed down because their congregations built homes in "more desirable" neighborhoods or districts, and when they moved out, another Jewish congregation moved in (at least for a while). This "hopscotching" occurred in a few instances in New York City, Chicago and elsewhere. Other times congregations built homes in suburbs not far from their urban origins, and even maintained the two locations for a certain amount of time. (Occasionally a Reform or Conservative congregation moved out of a synagogue and was replaced by an Orthodox group; but I am not designating those as "former" synagogues.)

In certain situations a congregation wishes to downsize from a large edifice, and moves out. In Queens, New York City, a congregation originally from the Lower East Side closed its summertime synagogue and built a newer, larger building on a major street, and vacated that smaller building on a side street– which was later turned into a private home. Occasionally a congregation decides that its older building is too much of a liability or requires too much renovation, and moves out to another site, either new or renovated for its own use.

Don't assume that these types of building closure situations are exclusive to the Jewish community: churches also have moved to other sites, or closed and merged, or simply shuttered for good. For example, in Brooklyn during the 2010s and early 2020s, I can think of at least five or six churches that were closed and demolished (although not without protestations from congregants and community members) and new buildings (residential, mixed use, non-profit) were built on the sites. This took place in Bay Ridge, western Park Slope, Bedford-Stuyvesant, near Brooklyn College; all are desirable areas, but the old church structures needed extensive repairs and faced dwindling attendance.

The American synagogues that have closed vary in size and architectural style, in condition and in religious rituals. Their names vary; many included the neighborhood in their name while others used strictly Hebrew titles. Most followed what is known as an Ashkenazic liturgy and fewer were Sephardic, but even within those broad categories, there were differences in prayer and song, customs and ceremonies. There were congregations that were identified (at least initially) as Polish, Russian, Hungarian, Iberian and with other nationalities and regions.

Each individual synagogue in the US that has closed has its own tale to tell. In some cases, the congregation removed all the Judaica, especially that which was particular to the congregation itself: memorial plaques, stained glass windows, site-specific pieces of artwork and craft, books, and other ritual items. Others left a lot of material, either because it was too difficult to remove the items or occasionally, because the congregants abandoned the building, even fled it.

I have walked into former synagogues in New York, New Jersey, Rhode Island, Pittsburgh, and elsewhere and noticed that the memorial plaques are completely intact. The stained glass windows remain (although many times they have suffered damage such as frame warpage, cracks in the glass, fading, and worse). The holy arks where the Torah scrolls had been stored are still in place on a dais (*bima*). Often these items were bolted to the walls, and I have seen synagogues in which the names of key congregants were etched into the walls, covered with paint (gold or black, for instance) and could not be removed. Whoever occupies the building next can either maintain these or cover them up.

The portable items are almost always removed, such as Torah scrolls, prayer books, prayer shawls, smaller artworks, and so on. Many times these items are donated to other active congregations or schools. Special care to rehome the Torah scrolls is almost always a given. People know that in the past, the Nazis and earlier the Crusaders and other enemies of the Jews would desecrate these Torah scrolls, ripping them to pieces and even burning them. Congregations that are closing do not want that fate to befall the Torah or Torahs that they have, so they are rehomed.

But other items are not so fortunate. On the first day of the demolition of a large former synagogue in Brooklyn, I was allowed inside to watch the workers just starting to undo the parts of the building. The heat and electricity were off (and it was quite cold inside the former Temple Isaac). Inside what had been the main sanctuary, the wooden pews were more or less placed where they had been for decades, although a few toward the back had been uprooted. Near the front of the airy space I saw pianos; three uprights, a few with sheet music from the church that had used the building after the synagogue moved out (Temple Isaac sort of merged with two other Brooklyn congregations, and the church left later on and seems to have merged with another congregation as well).

I asked a foreman if there were any plans for the pianos, and he shook his head. He even asked me if I wanted one; but I would need to bring my own crew to move it out. I tried playing them and each was out of tune, with broken keys and other damage. It saddened me (particularly as someone who took nine years of piano lessons) and I teared up, realizing they were going to be trashed. (Later on social media I let people know that the pianos were available but no one seemed interested in actually claiming them.)

At least one worker told me that part of the synagogue building was going to be retained and used in the construction of the new building. I had doubts about that but appreciated his telling me this. But I can say now that nothing seemed to be retained, and the new building that sits on that parcel of land does not at all resemble the former synagogue building.

This is another reason why I chose to document former synagogue buildings: as sad as it may be to see a former synagogue now functioning as a store or a church or a medical center, at least it is still standing and still being used, and can still be visited. Many other synagogues (and churches) have been demolished. All that is left of those are photographs, drawings, news stories, perhaps some memorabilia with the congregation's name on it that resides in a museum or library archive or a former member's attic (or in more fortuitous circumstances, has been rehomed in an active synagogue). Those are not *former* synagogues, those are completely *gone*, and to me that is even sadder.

For many generations one of the most important synagogues of the Lower East Side in Manhattan was the Beth Hamedrash Hagadol, commonly called the Norfolk Street Synagogue. It was built originally as a church. The synagogue had occupied the building since the 1880s and had modified it considerably. However, by the 1990s the congregation was quite small and the building had many structural problems, big and small. After Hurricane Irene it was deemed unsafe because windows had been blown out. Therefore it sat empty, until May 2017 when it fell victim to arson, set fire to by trespassing teenagers.

The building was thus a pitiful sight, yet there were rumors it would be rebuilt. Someone mentioned to me that construction work was going on, so I went to Manhattan to see what was going on. I asked a worker, and he told me that he heard it would be rebuilt. He seemed sincere, but I had my doubts. If you go to that site now, across from the chic Essex Market, you will see that the synagogue was not rebuilt, and a large modern building stands in its place.

I keep in mind the sad ends to both Temple Isaac and the Beth Hamedrash Hagadol when I conduct my research on former synagogues. I want to see if these sites will remain standing, even thrive, in their new incarnations. Sometimes the buildings get gussied up, but other times they deteriorate further. I feel affection for these buildings because they had been religious and social centers for so many Jews. They served communities for life-cycle events and weekly (even daily) prayer and learning. Friendships and family life took place within these sites.

There are people who will take a non-emotional point of view: they are just buildings. The people were on the move. The Torah scrolls and prayer books were given to other people who put them to use. You can't save every discarded synagogue. I know that, and I'm not looking to save them all. (Believe me, there are people who would like that to happen. But I know it's not practical.) That is why I do acknowledge those who take possession of the former synagogues, maintain them and use them so that they continue to live on in some form. These buildings help to tell the stories of Jewish communities throughout the United States.

What stories are told by former synagogues? Look at their synagogue names, carved into concrete or marble. Look at their cornerstones, which may have both secular and Hebrew years listed. Look at the congregants' names left inside, on memorial plaques and other types of displays, even the brass nameplates attached to pews. Look at the velvet coverings that might remain hanging or reused. Look at the windows. Look at the *mezuzah* (doorpost marker with religious parchment) at the doors (or their ghostly absence). Look at the reused schedule cases and other items.

People who conduct genealogical studies occasionally seek me out, asking if I have knowledge or contacts that can help with their research. They will query me about what are known as *landsmannschaften* synagogues, congregations that were begun by people from a particular town or city, mostly in Europe but occasionally with Middle Eastern roots. For example, I was contacted by a genealogist conducting research for a family with roots in Volozhin, rendered as Anshei Wolozin, a former synagogue on Madison Street in what is now Chinatown, lower Manhattan. Other times people have contacted me to ask if I have seen plaques that might remain in a former synagogue building, and if so, could I photograph it for them? (Sometimes that has worked out.) I am glad to help out people with this kind of roots and educational research.

Not everyone is pleased with the work I have been doing. There are two camps, in general, that have found fault with my field. First, there are the people who ask me with disdain, "Isn't it morbid to be researching and writing about closed synagogues?" Perhaps it is, but then you could say that about a lot of historical topics. Yes, studying former synagogues is often bittersweet. But I think of it as helping to answer questions, decipher past trends, and analyze an array of religious and sociological topics. I do enjoy "reading" a building, outside and inside, for clues to our past.

Another negative question with which I've dealt is framed as "Why are you airing the dirty laundry of Jews?" and occasionally "Why are you telling us about synagogues that became churches? This cannot happen!" First, discussing closed congregations is not necessarily damaging to Jewish communities. I will note that occasionally I have come across acrimonious closings, in which synagogues members fought against decisions to close. Yes, that has happened, I cannot deny that. A man once approached me to scold me about my explanations about a closed synagogue in the East Village of Manhattan; he complained that only "rebels" had told their side of the story. I cringed and thanked him for his opinion. But most of these synagogues closed because they couldn't be maintained or because the congregation built another home elsewhere. This does not equal "dirty laundry." It's reality, it's real estate, it's due to a host of factors.

The people who state that a synagogue cannot become a church or mosque or another type of religious site are basing their conclusions upon certain Jewish laws, but to an extent they don't understand them fully, and to an extent they are in denial. Like it or not, so many former synagogues have been deconsecrated and turned into churches, mosques and more. To those occasional naysayers I have said, take a look, see for yourself. Don't be in denial; I'm not lying about the changes that were rendered to these buildings.

In a nutshell, am I critical of the Jewish community at large if I study the many synagogues that have closed? No. Do we view former synagogues as failures? No, and that greatly oversimplifies the American Jewish experience. I have explained that "You can't force people to live in one place if they want to leave." American Jewish people, just like the majority of non-Jewish people, are not forced to live in one place, and not forced to upkeep one particular synagogue. Aside from the horrible histories of slavery and forced removals of Native American tribes, and taking into consideration economic and gender differences and sadly, even redlining, most Americans have been able to move around with a certain degree of fluidity. We are not bound to the land; as many have said to me "We're not in the ghetto" in the European ghetto sense, forced to reside in a Jewish district. Americans have long been known as a people on the move. Jewish people may gravitate to certain neighborhoods, but those boundaries can change over time, and they are largely voluntary moves.

And occasionally, on my Facebook page, I've been accused of lying about the mere fact that former synagogues (or "lost" synagogues, as I've often designated them) even exist as houses of worship for other religions. It is indisputable that many former synagogues become churches, typically for Protestant groups. A much smaller portion have become mosques or Hindu or Buddhist sites (and in at least one circumstance, the synagogue became a Messianic congregation). The sheer data proves that this happens, but a few have called into question my documentation. Why? Because there are intricate religious rules, officially, surrounding deconsecrating a Jewish house of worship. (See www.ritualwell.org and www.ccarnet.org for examples of this.)

If a crucifix is put up in a former synagogue building, some people view it as *avoda zara* (a form of idolatry). While this can be troubling, and painful to some people, it has happened again and again when one congregation leaves and another purchases a building with a sanctuary that seems desirable. (On the flip side, there are churches that close and have been bought up by synagogues. This is indisputable too.)

Just because someone is unhappy with the turn of events doesn't mean it didn't happen. History is quite often painful, messy, at odds with itself. This is true of American history, of Jewish history, of American-Jewish history.

The roots of my own interest in former synagogues began officially in 1999 on my birthday in April. On that day I didn't go to work, but instead drove around in the neighborhood of my early childhood. I brought along my 35mm SLR camera, a Minolta XG-M I had owned since 1981, loaded with black-and-white film, and set out to create a photographic essay.

As I drove around Flatbush, Brooklyn, I took note of a few curious things: the very first synagogue I attended as a tyke had turned into a Baptist church! Once known as Shaare Torah, it now sported a sign for Salem Missionary Baptist Church, even though there was still an unusual metal sculpture on the exterior, with "Shaare Torah" rendered in Hebrew letters. I also noticed other Judaica, including menorah designs on the fences. Shortly after taking photographs there, I drove over to the synagogue where my mother and my aunt had gone to Hebrew school (I'd found the address in a small prayer book my mom kept). I saw that what had been Kesser Torah in their childhood was now a church. I took photographs of the remaining details and Hebrew words.

Later that day I went to share a birthday cake with my parents, and I asked them frankly "Why didn't you tell me that Shaare Torah had become a church?" They looked pained and said nothing. I softened my tone and said "I realize it's kind of embarrassing, right?" I think it was Dad who then admitted that yes, the synagogue had closed and become a church. It was not a happy topic. But it sparked my interest in this subject. How many other synagogues in Brooklyn, in New York City, and elsewhere, had become churches, or medical centers (as had the synagogue where Dad celebrated his bar mitzvah ceremony) or schools (as had the synagogue that my mother-in-law had attended)? Did these buildings still have Judaica on the exteriors and in the interiors? Why did these synagogue buildings change so drastically?

My interest in lost synagogues grew beyond the borders of New York City, and during vacations I would notice former synagogues. People began contacting me to ask if I would document former synagogues in other parts of New York State, in New Jersey, and then elsewhere.

By delving into the topic of former synagogues throughout the United States, we can learn a great deal of Jewish history, American history, architectural and art history. We can play detective and learn how to "read" a building for its history. "Hidden history" comes to life. Adding to the store of knowledge is a chief goal in my life, as is helping people figure out how to learn and analyze. All those teacher courses and professional development opportunities thus paid off in multiple ways.

And then there is my great desire to write, and continue to write more. I have had six books published so far, including the three books covering The Lost Synagogues of New York City (Brooklyn in 2009, the Bronx and Queens in 2011, Manhattan and Staten Island in 2013). I also wrote

Walking Manhattan (published in 2015) and included information about former synagogues throughout Manhattan in that book. I have also written hundreds of articles and reviews, and penned essays that became chapters in five anthologies.

When searching for book topics, I realized that writing about lost synagogues was somewhat obscure but also something worthwhile, and a niche that was not over-saturated with book titles. When I was in graduate school for my MA in history, a fellow student once cracked a joke about "there are so many books about Abraham Lincoln, so do we really need more?" Keeping that in mind, I chose not to write a book about Mr. Lincoln, but instead about something that certainly deserved its own coverage. Not to put down Lincoln (I have long admired the man), but we could use more books about lost synagogues too.

What is the purpose of Former Synagogues in the United States? Is it a travel guide? (Yes, certainly.) My intentions have been to do much more than merely list the names of former synagogues, provide basic pertinent data and photographs, and allow readers to reminisce. Beyond that, I want this book to show the history and stories of many places; to explore the similarities and differences among many of these sites, not only within a town or city but across state lines; to delve into the architecture, decorative art and elements of synagogues in different parts of the United States. I have discerned similarities between former synagogues in Chicago and Cleveland, Detroit and New Jersey, Rhode Island and upstate New York, and elsewhere. Clearly there are differences but there are also central themes and quirky coincidences.

I have greatly enjoyed visiting various places throughout the US, studying these buildings, and analyzing their stories. I hope readers will too. But I also have this lingering feeling that I can never truly stop documenting these sites. There is always another that I could find, or more data or more first-person narratives. An example: one day one of my page followers sent me a photograph of a former synagogue in a small Pennsylvania town, Mahanoy City. This lost shul, the Beth Israel Congregation at 300 West Mahanoy Street, was actually for sale. Long empty, someone on Facebook was trying to sell the building for $80,000. The site was at least three hours away from me, but immediately I began to ponder a visit, and wonder what other lost synagogues I could add on to make the excursion worth the effort. Just seeing the photograph of this distressed brick building, which still featured a sign with its name rendered in Hebrew, began to haunt me.

In addition, I have not had the time (yet) to visit lost synagogues in every town, city and state throughout the United States. I do feel badly about this, and perhaps will write another volume about this topic with former synagogues in Maine, and Alabama, and so on.

As you read this book and study the photographs, you might realize that you have seen some of these buildings and wondered about their pasts. Perhaps you have seen a former synagogue in a locale that I did not cover here. You might even know one or more of these sites, either when they were still synagogues or afterward (or both). If you can contribute to the store of knowledge about former synagogues, please make it known. Or perhaps you know about a former church, and you can help to tell its story. My work is also meant to serve as a catalyst for other, related fields of research.

Hopefully you will appreciate these buildings to some extent. I have met many people who reminisce or learn about their family histories through learning about former synagogues. Others have enjoyed learning about art and architecture, culture, and much more.

A special note about the NYC Department of Finance Address Search feature: you can find out the size of the building and other factors, such as the current estimated market value, from the website search. This was updated greatly sometime in 2024: now it is easier to locate buildings on the page. You can type in the address, and the layout of the results for each address is easier to understand. In addition, now there is a thumbnail photo (and clickable) for the building, and you can also find out the Year Built for a building and often, the primary construction material (masonry, reinforced concrete, stone, for example). This information is helpful, and I wish that there were more websites such as this one.

# Acknowledgements

This book and related projects would not exist without the help offered to me by family and friends, colleagues, and people who only know me as "the lost synagogues lady". In a myriad of ways, people have given me information on locations, have allowed me to interview them, steered me toward useful resources, and much more.

Many people have assisted me in my research into Former Synagogues. A number of these people did so in a casual manner, others more formally. Some acted as sounding boards for my ideas and concerns. Others offered resources and tips on particular sites (including those about to close or be demolished). There are people listed here whom I have known for decades, and others for a handful of years. Several have sent me data and photographs, links to worthwhile articles and essays, while others reminisced about particular lost synagogues and other Jewish institutions.

A few have been quite inspirational, and I owe a huge debt of gratitude to a few who gave me breaks and inspiration. In this category I place *Frank Jump,* for creating a lovely page that displayed my early photographs, Frank H. Jump presents Ellen Levitt's Former Synagogues of Brooklyn ( which you can find online at https://www.fadingad.com/Levitt/). Then there is the late *Gary Mokotoff* of www.avotaynu.com for publishing my trilogy of New York City Lost Synagogues books; thank you for believing in my work.

Thank you to the late professor and writer *William Helmreich,* whose books about New York City inspired me as far as content and style. When I met him at the Brooklyn Book Festival in 2019, we had a wonderful conversation about my topic ("We have to talk!" he said to me boisterously when I introduced myself to him at the Princeton University Press table.) He also included my Lost Synagogues books in the bibliography of one of his books. A special thank you to the amazing and extraordinarily talented *Alex Harsley* of 4th Street Photo Gallery. He knows New York City in such a special manner, and is one of the most intriguing photographers you could ever meet. A great mentor in all ways.

A general thank you to my family and friends for listening to me, reminiscing, offering ideas and advice. Howard, Jessica, Michelle, my brother Ben, Lauren, Josh and Rob, my cousins Willie and Robert, Molly, Nora and Daniel. And to my parents Leah and Edward, and my aunt Miriam, I wish you knew how much your help meant to me. Also thanks to my late in-laws Janet and Bob Dankowitz, and to Bev Dankowitz, Dani and Ari.

Bennett Katz, Charlie Hall, Noah Levine of Jewish Community Legacy Project. Steven DuBois, Matthew Christopher of Abandoned America. Professor Samuel Gruber, Robb Packer (Chicago former synagogues expert). Members of the BJHI (Brooklyn Jewish Historical Initiative) especially Howard Teich, Sarina Roffe, Joe Dorinson, Ron Schweiger and Raul Rothblatt. Sergey Kandinsky, Charles Bowe, Steve Lasky, Tony Carnes, Blair Staten, Jacob Scheer, Damian Rose, for much information on vacant shul sites. Mark Nazimova, Art Finkel, Curtis Bolden in Queens. Rabbi Shlomo Segal, Kevin Walsh, Grace How, Lori Pandolfo, Heather O'Mara, Members of Tora Dojo Association and their insights. East Bronx History Forum, especially Anthony Pisciotta, Rich Vitacco, Rabbi Moshe Fuchs, Edwin German, Elliot Schechter, Peretz Zvi Davidson, Rachael Spero Shaul. Members of the FJC, Flatbush Jewish Center, especially Mike Levine for reminiscing about Shaare Torah and Brooklyn in general, and Sara Sloan, Daniel Soyer, Larry Margarik, Scott Stein, Dina Garfinkel, Elisabeth Epstein, Shoshanna and David Cooper, Rabbi Lev Meirowitz Nelson and Eliana Meirowitz, Rabbi Heather Miller, and the others. Brad Kolodny of the Jewish Historical Society of Long Island www.jhsli.org. Harold Kravis, Arieh Lebowitz, Phil Yourish, Max Herman regarding New Jersey. FWDG (Flatbush Women's Davening Group) members, especially Barbara Mazor, Lynne Cassouto, Jennifer Horowitz and especially Shulamith Berger in her role as Curator of Special Collections at Yeshiva University's Mendel Gottesman Library.

Rose Adler, George Bodarky (WFUV), Hillel Alon, Wendy and Stacey Cahn. My photography teachers at Murrow High School, especially Mr. C. Reece and Mr. G. Tobin; and photography insights from my former classmates Erik Lieber and Ben Russell, Brad Goz, Alex Bowe DeRosa for information on Toledo, Ohio sites. Shelley Miller Braff and Mike Braff, Ron Z, Rabbi Moshe Plotkin, Charles Endelman. Nico Collazzo and Mario Perez, two of my former high school students who told me about specific sites in the Bronx and Westchester. Marta Braiterman Tanenbaum, Penina

Goldstein, Edward Lapa, Shimon Sieskel, Toby Goldfarb Weiner, Sandra Martin, Laura O'Keefe, Rona N. Birnbaum, Joanna Barouch, JD Arden, Diane Witek, Leo Finston, Mindy and Mark Weinblatt, Georgette Asherman, Cindy Mazer, Josh Sayer, Jacqui and Barry Elkayam, Barry Shapiro and Robin Kaufman, Miriam Wolff, Lisa Joseph Rothman, Jodi Sadowsky Dillon, Audrey Zimring of the Staten Island UFT for having me give lectures online about lost synagogues.

Special thanks to Dvorah Kaplan, for sending me information about Passaic and other locales, and for helping me to select photographs.

Special thanks to Adam from Sysut Computers, for his technical help.

And thank you to so many other people, some whose names I never knew.

# Research, Travel, Photography and Writing About Former Synagogues

Throughout my documentation of former synagogues in my local region and then in other parts of the United States, I have put great emphasis not only on writing about them but also on photographing the exteriors and often the interiors of these buildings. There are really four major aspects of my work: research, travel, photography, and writing. All are important and I find satisfaction working within each realm.

Research comes first, especially for addresses and travel routes, but also throughout the process, in order to gain more insight into the individual lost synagogues and to form a larger picture of them, to see the network of other sites within which they belong.

In the early years of my research, especially from 2005 onward, I made use of both traditional and contemporary sources. I began at the Central Library in Brooklyn, going through old phone books and reference books in their Brooklyn history room (which has since expanded). I viewed microfilm and spoke with people who could identify and reminisce about former synagogues in Brooklyn, Manhattan and later in Queens and the Bronx.

I forget who suggested that I visit the Municipal Archives in the City Hall area of Manhattan, and comb through the WPA (Works Progress Administration) 1939–1940 Survey of Houses of Worship. This was part of the WPA Federal Writers' Project and Historical Records Survey. I spent hours going through the microfilm (and later found parts of it online) to find information on old synagogues throughout New York City: names and addresses, clergy members, numbers of Torah scrolls, and other data. There were other records and resource books I consulted there, in the beautiful old building at 31 Chambers Street.

I found other helpful websites online, some by recommendation, some by poking around or asking questions. I visited the archive at the New York Public Library, known as the Dorot Jewish Division, and found other useful documents in the Reading Room and Archives there.

I also spent time in the JTS (Jewish Theological Seminary) archives, and later in the YU (Yeshiva University) Archives and Special Collections, especially with the help of Shulamith Berger.

I also used my two professional Facebook pages to request information from people who were interested in former synagogues. The first was The Lost Synagogues of New York City and NJ, and after that one was hacked badly, I created Former Synagogues of NY, NJ and the US. I truly appreciate the help my followers and friends have offered.

Travel is also very important: I have often visited these sites by driving to them, but in some cases I have traveled to them by bicycle or by taking mass transit, almost always subway trains. And I have visited most of the New York City area former synagogues more than once; there are several that I pass by regularly when I travel around Brooklyn, and I always take notice of their condition. They are like old friends that I greet warmly.

As someone who has long enjoyed working with maps, the travel planning has often been a fun aspect of my work. (To me, maps are a category of artwork, a crossroads of craft with history and planning.) In the early years, I made constant use of my spiral Hagstrom New York City map book, marking it up with a series of dots, lines, notes, highlighting and such. This way I not only plotted out my routes, but also I was able to see how concentrated lost synagogues were in certain areas such as Brownsville, Brooklyn; the South Bronx; the East Village in Manhattan; and elsewhere. I also used the Mapquest website in the early years, but in the last several years I have used Google Maps almost exclusively. I have created a series of *My Maps*, a few of which span not just cities but states.

Driving around Brooklyn and other parts of New York City is usually easy for me, but as I have ventured further out, the drives have gotten longer and I feel more pressure to find enough places to document. I do feel disappointment when I arrive at an address and realize that the building I had hoped to see is gone; if it is in New York City it's not a big deal but if I have driven hours for naught (and that has happened a few times), it is a greater disappointment. That is why I have also used the Map View feature so much in recent years.

Several times I combined my search for lost synagogues with vacations, or with travel for other writing assignments, or with social visits. During vacation excursions to places such as San Francisco, Cleveland, Las Vegas, New Orleans, and the Washington, DC area, I have carved out time to find lost synagogues. When I wrote for a website called Music & Sound Retailer, I visited cities or regions to review musical instrument stores– and during some trips I also visited lost synagogues (such as my trips to Syracuse, the Hudson Valley, Providence and elsewhere). At times I brought along a family member or a friend who was curious, such as when I brought my dad along in Bed-Stuy, Brooklyn and Manhattan's Lower East Side, or brought along my former student and friend Nico to see Westchester and Bronx former synagogues,

A few of my trips were full-day excursions with a lot of driving (Baltimore, the Capital District of New York State, parts of New Jersey, Philadelphia) but I have taken a few lengthier trips. My most ambitious trip was in early July 2023, when I drove to upstate New York (including Rome, Oneonta, Rochester and Buffalo) into Erie, Pennsylvania, then to Detroit, and to small cities in Ohio, to Cleveland, and then home to Brooklyn. That was a rapid four-night trip with an immense amount of driving. (I encountered two heavy rainstorms as I drove east during that trip, and there were nerve-wracking moments.)

Photography has long been one of my greatest passions. Mom gave me a 126 Kodak camera for my ninth birthday, and I adored it (and would constantly nag her for film packs). Then for another birthday I asked for a 35mm camera, and I went with Mom to purchase a Konica with a fixed lens. I used that for a few years until my most precious camera purchase, made after the summer of 1981. I took all the money I earned as a day camp counselor and bought a Minolta XGM, a 35 mm camera, and later on bought additional lenses for it. I have used that camera ever since for most of my film photographs (aside from inexpensive gimmick cameras such as the quadrant camera and a fixed fish-eye lens camera).

I have also used digital cameras, because it has become almost impossible not to work with these for projects. I have used a pocket-sized Canon PowerShot ELPH 160 for its portability, my various cell phone cameras, and a Canon EOS Rebel T5 that is a hand-me-down from my younger daughter.

I mention the cameras because I'm a gear nerd, and have put these various cameras to different uses. In many cases I would take photographs of lost synagogues with more than one camera at each visit: the cell phone camera pictures to post on Facebook, the digital pictures for publishing and to catch more detail, and the film cameras (loaded with black-and-white film) to make enlargements of some for exhibition.

My years at Edward R. Murrow High School were instrumental in my practical photography knowledge because I took Photography classes here. I took a year of black-and-white darkroom photography, and a half year in color printing.These classes taught me so much about darkroom work, about composition, experimentation, and so much more. I would not be where I am today without these courses. I learned even more when I taught photography, as a course and as a club, at two schools (Manhattan Comprehensive Night High School and Murry Bergtraum HS).

I have photographed a wide variety of subjects, but I take particular pride and find fulfillment with my many photographs of lost synagogues. This is a combination of artistic exploration, devotion to documenting these buildings, a sense of educating people about the topic, and a need to promote the work in an engaging, visual manner. If I only wrote about them, the former synagogues would not be nearly as interesting to most people; by taking photographs and sharing them with the public, I get more people interested in the subject. In turn many ask questions about them and engage with them on various levels.

These photographs can elicit deep emotions in some folks, and at times people are saddened, even irritated or angered by them. People ponder the shifts in the Jewish communities, due to what they see in these photos. My photographs and writing are meant not just to be dry, academic exercises but are intended to touch people's emotions. I want people to ask questions, and do their own research in the field.

A group of the earliest of these photos, a set of black-and-white framed photographs, were part of an exhibition at what was then called the Brooklyn Historical Society (now the Center for Brooklyn History, and even earlier it was the Long Island Historical Society). Located in downtown Brooklyn, I was thrilled to have my photographs of Brooklyn lost synagogues selected for exhibition in their gallery. They gave me a stipend to frame the photographs, hosted an opening night for the work, and I also delivered a lecture about the photos and the subject.

I've spoken about "my subject" elsewhere since that time in November-December 2006, but this was a special occasion and I felt that it brought extra respect to my work. Photography can seem so mundane and omnipresent, but at times it takes on an elevated position and that happened with my initial set of photos. After that I gave lectures on lost synagogues at the Center for Jewish History in Manhattan, at several synagogues, at the East Bronx History Forum, and online for the UFT Retirees program.

When you see a photograph of a former synagogue, you look at it as a whole, then you can focus on specific details. Are you drawn to the size? The condition? The artistic details? The use of English or Hebrew? The recognizable Judaica? The clash of remaining Judaica with the current elements of a church, a medical center, a school, and so on? Does the photo illustrate a story? Do you wonder about how it has changed over time? Do you compare it to other synagogues you have seen? (I do, certainly.)

# Safety While Documenting Lost Synagogues

While scouting out and documenting former synagogues, especially in cities and certain "tougher" neighborhoods, I have often traveled throughout and around areas that have higher crime rates. I have been aware of and careful about this, yet sometimes people have warned me about these areas, and even urged me not to go to these precincts.

For the most part I have shrugged off the warnings, and chalked them up to hypersensitivity, and to some extent to latent or even overt racism. Many of the areas where there are lost synagogue buildings were previously heavily Jewish but are now populated heavily by People of Color, especially Black people and Latino people. In some of the areas there are South Asians and other groups.

I am aware of what I usually dub, in a detached manner, the "changing demographics" of sections of cities, towns and suburbs. Some call it "the color line." Others have nastier terms for this, but we could also call these areas "the 'hood." ("Ghetto" is one of the milder and older terms for these areas.)

I first began my work in Brooklyn, where I would drive around places such as Brownsville, East New York, Bedford-Stuyvesant and New Lots. Bed-Stuy in recent years has become much more diverse and parts of the neighborhood are quite gentrified. But even in Brownsville and East New York, and nearby New Lots, which all have long-time reputations of being gritty, there has been a lot more new construction and renovation in recent years. These areas do have higher crime rates, but I have never faced any such problems. (However, one time I hit a pothole on a street in East New York, and the sharp impact caused my car trunk to fly open. Another time in ENY a man driving a small truck backed into my car and gave it a dent; he apologized and his insurance covered the repair.)

After that I went into parts of the Bronx and Queens that have been considered more dangerous. I have never had a problem there, but perhaps because I am a lifelong New Yorker, this hasn't fazed me. Even the occasional forward panhandler has not rattled my nerves.

Going further afield from New York City, I have been much more aware of higher-crime sections of certain neighborhoods. New Jersey cities such as Newark and Paterson are now largely non-white, but I did not have any problems. In fact, I have studied Newark over the years and it has undergone much more renovation and new construction, its fortunes improving.

The first place where I felt somewhat more afraid was Camden, New Jersey. The first time I drove out there I saw a lot of abandoned buildings, and at the bus depot, where I used the restroom, I encountered people who were nodding off from taking drugs. I stayed calm and had no trouble.

Since then I have traveled to places with reputations that do frighten many people: parts of Philadelphia beyond the tourist sections; residential areas of Detroit, Baltimore and Cleveland; even parts of northern New York such as Buffalo and Rochester. I have always stayed alert, and on the rare occasion when I sensed trouble brewing, I drove away and returned later, when things seemed safer.

One of the few incidents when I did feel unsafe and angered, was in the North Lawndale neighborhood of Chicago, in mid-November 2023. While driving on South Keeler Avenue, I spotted a lost synagogue, stopped my rental car and took a photograph from my seat. Suddenly I heard a "thump" sound, and saw a man attempting to open my rear passenger side door.The door was locked, but I slammed on the gas and screamed out a few curse words. This unnerved me, and it was memorable, but it was the sole scary incident that I faced.

If I want to document these former synagogue buildings in person, I need to travel to them and walk around them, or at least view them from the relative comfort of my car's driver seat. Whenever I encounter local residents, I am polite and respectful. In so many cases they have not only been polite to me, they have actually asked me in-depth questions and reminisced about the buildings, providing me with more useful information.

I have made a point of being as calm and respectful as possible partly in response to the somewhat (in my opinion) denigrating comments a few other Jewish researchers have said or written. One man who created a website of former synagogues in the Bronx wrote blunt, unkind things (in my humble estimation) about the Black people who moved into the Bronx.

Another Jewish writer, with whom I have spoken a few times, said scathing things about the lost synagogues he has seen throughout New York City. In contrast, the late Professor William Helmreich told me that was always personable with the people he encountered, no matter their race or ethnicity, and I have striven to follow his lead.

To a lesser extent, I have also faced unsafe physical plant conditions in some lost synagogues: a few have had broken flooring, warped and deteriorating steps and stairs, inside and out. Then I have had to be concerned about my balance and preventing falls and other dangers.

A few times I entered abandoned synagogue buildings and came face to face with clearly dangerous conditions. The last time I walked inside the former Harlem site of Ohab Zedek (which I wrote about in my book The Lost Synagogues of Manhattan, 2013) I saw safety signs requiring hard hats; it was in the process of being demolished. I had a bicycle helmet so I wore that in lieu of a hard hat.

I visited twice in the former Temple Isaac in Prospect Heights, Brooklyn and saw dangerous conditions: the first time I had thought it was occupied (then quickly realized that it wasn't) and almost tripped twice on the deteriorating floor of the basement level. The second time a man arranged for me to visit inside the first day that a crew had begun to demolish the building, a process that took a few months. It was quite mournful to me and I was saddened to see three pianos that were going to be demolished along with the building.

Perhaps the two scariest instances of physical plant danger were those I dealt with in early July 2023. On July 4th I crept quietly inside the former B'nai Israel on Joseph Avenue in Rochester, New York. The building was in shambles, and I narrowly missed walking into at least one sinkhole and then noticed a second. That was alarming and I scurried back quickly. The second time was two days later in Detroit, at an abandoned former synagogue on Blaine Avenue. I walked around to the back of the building and got inside briefly but then realized that much of the first floor had rotted away. I shuddered and left the building quickly.

Another factor that was not quite dangerous but still made me uncomfortable was the few occasions when I did not feel welcome inside a building. Almost any time I have entered a lost synagogue, be it in NYC or elsewhere, people have been kind to me. A few times they asked me to return a bit later after the sermon or the Sunday school session, and I did so. But one time in the New Lots section of Brooklyn, at a lost synagogue that had been turned into a church, a woman peppered me with questions about why I wanted to come inside. Then she began snapping at me because she assumed that I was "in real estate" and wanted to try to purchase the building. I told her no but she was growing angrier at me, so I left the building, rather than getting into an argument. A similar incident happened to me once in the Bronx.

I suppose the people thought that the only reason a woman like me would be interested in the building was in order to buy it and kick them out. I was thus seen as a dreaded gentrifier.

On the other hand, there were two times when congregants were quite nice to me but I experienced discomfort because I realized that there were open caskets in the sanctuary. One time in a beautiful former shul in Newark, New Jersey and one time in Cleveland, I walked inside the buildings and chatted with congregants, and then realized that a funeral was going to commence shortly. I stayed calm and each time I was allowed to take photographs inside the building.

Two other safety factors I have faced, sadly common to nearly everyone who drives, are bad drivers (wreckless, entitled, impaired, inattentive) and adverse traffic conditions such as poorly paved roads, severe weather, non-working lights, and the like. In Chicago I dealt with at-grade trains that did not have properly working safety gates. While driving through Ohio, Pennsylvania, New Jersey and New York, on more than one occasion, I maneuvered through heavy rain, fog, hail and snow. A few times I cut short my trips or sections of them, due to bad weather. I've learned how to juggle an umbrella and a camera when desperate to snap photos of a particular former synagogue.

I have also kept in mind the time of day when on excursions, because the setting sun not only makes it harder to snap quality photographs, but it also brings on safety concerns, especially in areas with which I have scant familiarity. I am hyper-aware of safety and conditions when I have gone to take photographs and make visits, especially when I have been outside of New York City. But I do my best also to be open minded and keep a positive attitude. For the most part, I have met so many pleasant people, seen many interesting places, and learned a great deal. In doing so, I want to share those positive experiences with my readers.

# From the New York City Core Outward to the United States

There are approximately 250–300 standing former synagogues throughout the five boroughs of New York City, and more can also be found all around the United States. My general perspective and understanding of former synagogues started with my knowledge of those located throughout New York City, and initially Brooklyn. As a lifelong resident of New York City, and specifically Brooklyn, my frame of reference has been my hometown. I have seen congregations close their buildings, merge with others, shutter altogether. I have driven past many of these buildings countless times, on my way to work, shop, do activities, and visit family and friends.

New York City does loom large and significant in the history of American Jews, if not global Jewry overall. Colonial Nieuw Amsterdam housed the first Jewish community in what would eventually become the United States. Before the late 1800s New York had a sizable Jewish community, and from the late 1800s onward, when the celebrated large waves of immigration came from Central and Eastern Europe and elsewhere, New York housed the largest concentration of Jewish people in the United States. It still has the largest outside of Israel, even if the internal concentrations have shifted somewhat.

But I realized over time, for many reasons, that I should expand my coverage of documentation of lost and former synagogue buildings. I had been casually seeking out former shul buildings and related Jewish buildings when I vacationed elsewhere in the US, and could not help but compare the architecture, the layout, the names, and other elements to the Greater New York buildings I had seen. I also grew interested in comparing urban synagogues to suburban, large city to smaller city former synagogues, early 1900s to later construction, and other aspects.

My "New York Centric" frame of reference needed to expand, and my curiosity was rewarded. Part of this was due also to my giving tours within New York City, mostly walking tours but also a few bike tours and bus and car tours. Some people who joined these tours would tell me about former (and active) synagogues with which they were familiar in places such as Philadelphia, Baltimore, Long Island and elsewhere.

The first city I became particularly interested in documenting, aside from New York City, was Newark, New Jersey. In the mid 2010s I began to meet people who belonged to an old but revived Newark synagogue, Ahavas Sholom, at 145 Broadway. One of their members, Harold Kravis, had joined a lost synagogues bike tour I gave in Brooklyn. He and a few other members of Ahavas Sholom, which also houses the Jewish Museum of New Jersey, encouraged me to look at former synagogues in the downtown area as well as the Weequahic neighborhood and beyond, and post about them on my Lost Synagogues page. I did, and became very interested in Newark's lost shuls. I noticed similarities with buildings in New York City, but also noted how the city had different experiences than New York, especially from the 1960s onward. In fact, I helped them to conduct research for a fascinating museum exhibition.

Another person who really got me thinking about this was a young woman named Rachael Spero Shaul, who joined two of my tours in Manhattan. She then encouraged me to create a walking tour of former synagogues in the Washington Heights region of Manhattan. I decided to do so and she helped out with planning and getting our group access to a particular old synagogue building that was barely hanging on. (I surprised her at the end of the tour by giving her a portion of the tour proceeds.)

Rachael is originally from Cleveland and had told me about shuls out there; so had my friend Jacqui, who also grew up near that area. In 2014 I visited Cleveland with my older daughter Jessica, primarily to spend time at the Rock and Roll Hall of Fame and the nearby Cedar Point Amusement park in Sandusky. But one morning of this short vacation I drove around a few neighborhoods of Cleveland, with notes and addresses culled from internet research, and I photographed a few former synagogues. (Rachael later created a van tour of former synagogues in Cleveland and I was very pleased by her work.) I realized that I should conduct research of former synagogues in other parts of the country, not only to understand their communities, but also to understand my own hometown, and American Jewry in general.

Yet another person I met is someone whose name I do not recall. But I spoke with him at a Purim holiday luncheon (March 2023) in my neighborhood. A neighbor had invited me to lunch on Purim day, and on a whim I took him up on his offer. Before we all sat down to his family's lavish meal, I chatted with someone in his circle, a man in his 70s who had grown up in Detroit. I told him I was considering a visit to Detroit to document former synagogues, and he reminisced about his years there. It dawned on me that I had only been to the midwest briefly, a trip to Chicago and the short vacation to Cleveland, and I grew more curious about the Jewish communities in this part of the US.

Lastly, one of the more inspirational people I met, and who was interested in my work, was the late Professor William Helmreich. A sociologist and author of ten books, I found out that he had listed two of my books in the bibliography for his wonderful work The New York Nobody Knows (2013). I enjoyed that one, as well as The Brooklyn Nobody Knows (2016) and I got to meet him at one of the academic publisher tables at the Brooklyn Book Festival in 2019. We had a lively discussion and he also stopped by later on to visit my group's table, the Brooklyn Jewish Historical Initiative. I deeply admired his writing style, academic yet approachable, and told him so. He encouraged me to visit other cities and suburbs, to document their former synagogues and schools. Sadly, he was one of the people I knew who died early on during the COVID-19 Pandemic.

I do enjoy traveling in other parts of the country to see these former synagogues in person. I have visited many but not all such buildings, and I look forward to continuing this study in the years to come. But I was very eager and gratified to visit places such as Detroit, Pittsburgh and Philadelphia, northern New York, and towns in Connecticut, to compare and contrast the lost synagogues of these areas to those in New York City. I also revisited certain places such as Cleveland and San Francisco, in order to see these sights with a greater understanding.

I will begin this study with coverage of several New York City former synagogues and institutions that I missed covering in the original book trilogy, beginning with Brooklyn, moving onto the Bronx, and Queens. Following that I will move further around New York State: Long Island (Nassau and Suffolk Counties), Yonkers and Westchester, the Catskills and the Capital District, into Central, Northern and Western New York, including Kingston, Schenectady, Albany, Syracuse, Rome, Oswego, Rochester and Buffalo.

The states nearest to New York are next: New Jersey and Connecticut, and Pennsylvania. Of particular importance are Newark and its suburbs, and Philadelphia. Next we will look at Ohio, especially Cleveland, and then to Michigan with a focus on Detroit. We will venture over to Baltimore. Then the field becomes more spread out, with sites in New Orleans, Seattle, San Francisco.

I did not visit every single lost synagogue that is standing; this would have been beyond my means and energy. I will mention other cities and sites, and I certainly acknowledge their existence, but I could not find every single one. I contend that what is included in this book is certainly a highly representative assortment of former synagogues.

These synagogues range in size, as far as the buildings themselves and the lots and even campuses. They stand in cities, suburbs, towns, and even in more rural areas. Some are in excellent shape, some are in decent condition, and others are decrepit. Among the oldest are former synagogue buildings that date to the 1860s and 1870s. Many were built during the 1920s, but others were constructed in the 1950s and later. There are even former shul buildings that date to the 1970s.

Many of these buildings have become houses of worship for other religions and faiths, especially Christian (and Protestant) denominations, but others now serve as mosques, meditation centers, Hindu sites. Others serve as schools or as parts of college campuses. Others have become private residences, community and cultural centers, medical offices, and so on. And there are a few that were abandoned when I saw them.

There are some former synagogues that I have been able to visit several times over the past several years, and I have noted how some have changed while others barely do. For example, for at least seven years I have photographed a former synagogue at 928 DeKalb Avenue in Brooklyn. I had not known about it for the 2009 book but have since been to see it from outside at least ten times, and was inside once. The most drastic change that I have noticed is that it had been a church but later became a mosque. There is more or less the same amount of Judaica on the exterior, but the faiths since then have changed.

Another is the former Bayside Jewish Center building in Queens. I visited it shortly after the Jewish congregation decamped, and the Korean Community Center moved in. I have visited there at least four times, and each time less and less exterior Judaica remained visible. As of early September 2023, I only noticed a cornerstone with Jewish symbols, as well as the designs of remaining stained glass sanctuary windows from the outside.

In mentioning these two sites, I want to show that former synagogue buildings do not necessarily stay in one manner, or with one use. There is a former synagogue in Syracuse that is now a hotel, but earlier it had served as an arts center. Just as synagogues can become former synagogues, they can also change as time goes by. What will the future bring to these sites? Will they change hands again? Will they change from, say, being used as a church to becoming a medical center or a nursery school?

And yes, I have actually come across at least one former synagogue/Jewish school that became a secular school, and then became a Jewish school once again! The site to which I am referring is in Brooklyn, on Willoughby Avenue in Bed-Stuy. Will this be a major trend? I do not think so, but it can happen, depending upon one of my favorite terms, "shifting demographics."

There are certainly things unique to the Jewish community of New York City, particularly due to its large size and lengthy pedigree. But I have tried my best to be open to many other parts of the US, to look at their communities, their lost synagogues and Jewish institutions, and learn about the circumstances of their regions. This has helped me to deal with my own bias, to learn more about how Jews interact with and establish themselves in various communities. As a former public high school social studies teacher, I have also been curious about seeing other parts of the US and finding common ground. In the process of learning about various Jewish communities, I have also learned more about the United States overall. It is a humbling process and I intend to continue beyond the scope of this book.

One more point of comparison: I have traveled to several cities in Europe, and have made a point of visiting their synagogues. Sometimes I went inside to attend a religious service, as I did in Prague, Madrid, Paris, Lisbon and Florence. A few times I visited these synagogues and the museums located inside them, as well as historic cemeteries and galleries (Budapest, Prague, Amsterdam). Other times I was only able to see these buildings from the outside, as in parts of London, Istanbul, and elsewhere.

I always looked carefully at the styles of these synagogues and looked for comparisons and contrasts with those American synagogues with which I was familiar. For one thing, the archetypal "wooden folk synagogue" is a style I have not seen in the United States. Found in parts of Central and Eastern Europe, this style seems to have only vaguely traveled across the oceans.

Other elements of European shuls have been recreated in American shul buildings: for example, the Dohany Street Synagogue (Budapest) style of towers and windows can be seen in certain American synagogues. I have seen synagogues in Paris that were similar to some in New York City. The stark modernity of the Beth Yaacov Synagogue in Paris can be spotted in some urban and suburban American shuls of the late 20th century.

The dome is one design element that can be seen in certain European synagogues as well as those in the United States. Stained glass windows are also common to many synagogues in the Old World as well as the New World.

One of the bigger differences I have noticed about many of the European synagogues I visited, especially those that are known for the historic and tourist appeal, is how they are located on streets. Several are set on urban squares, and do not always allow for cars and other vehicles to pull up right beside them. This is very different from so many urban American synagogues, which have actual sidewalks running in front of the buildings and lawns, if they are present. I can not recall seeing a European synagogue that had a parking lot adjacent to the property, as I have seen in many suburban and small town synagogues, even some urban ones. In a few European locales, the synagogues have been located on narrow streets, almost tucked away. I would venture to say that a few former shuls in Philadelphia could compare in that manner.

Many things account for these similarities and differences, certainly. Styles come and go and reappear in variations. Finances figure in. Zoning laws vary from place to place. But much of this can also be chalked up to the nebulous factor of identity. How do the many Jewish congregations hope to express their identities? In fanciful and exotic manners or more down to earth appearances? People involved in the building committees long ago may have had different goals than congregants who join several decades later. Laws about the placement of cemeteries certainly have changed over time, so that urban synagogues in the US do not often have cemeteries adjacent to their properties. The oldest continuous congregation in the US, Congregation Shearith Israel in Manhattan, has three small cemeteries spread around lower Manhattan but they are not near the current location on Central Park West (which has been in use since 1897).

I may have started my study with my hometown of New York City, but went way beyond, in order to understand much of the American Jewish experience. If we consider houses of worship and schools to be of core importance to Jewish communal life, we also must look at the former, lost synagogues. They reveal much of the story as well.

# Former Synagogues Can Change Over Time

They don't always remain the same:

Their appearances can change (paint jobs, additions built, signs removed, deterioration, stained glass windows removed or amended, roof work, and more)

They can be turned into a church and then a mosque (DeKalb Avenue)

They can be turned into a secular school and then a Jewish school (Willoughby Avenue)

They can be a church, then another church, then become abandoned (Blaine Street in Detroit)

They can be changed into a church and then an event space (B'nai Jeshurun in Newark, NJ)

They can become a church, become abandoned and then get knocked down (Prospect Place)

They can be vandalized, then be renovated, and so on. There is not one specific template.

Certainly, many do follow a typical path of usage: from synagogue to church; synagogue to private residence; synagogue to school. But not all, and there are quite a number of variations.

The former synagogues that I document here may very likely change more. As time goes on, these buildings may find new uses, or may be knocked down. In each individual listing I write about what I have seen in person, and sometimes photographs online, books or library archives, for comparison. Many of these buildings I visited only once (especially if they are outside of New York City, Long Island and certain New Jersey cities) but others I revisited twice or even multiple times. I want to document and describe what they are at a particular moment and have the reader see something of their past and present.

When I have brought up the subject of former synagogue buildings, of lost synagogues and Jewish institutions that have been repurposed, people have differing opinions and emotions. Often they feel bittersweet, nostalgic, sad, a yearning to revisit the building if they had a personal relationship with it (through their own past experiences or those of family members).

Occasionally people have grown disgusted or even angry because they view the repurposed buildings with a sense of betrayal. Why did the Jewish community leave this building and others in the vicinity? As I have written elsewhere, there are many reasons for that.

Sometimes people express embarrassment. This is actually one of the first reactions I encountered when I began to explore this topic in April 1999. On my birthday I took the day off from work and drove around my Flatbush, in Brooklyn, where I had spent my earliest years. I stopped by my old synagogue and saw that it was now a Baptist church; so was the nearby synagogue which my mom and aunt had attended. So were at least three other nearby shuls, now former shuls. That evening I had dinner and birthday cake with my parents and asked them if they knew that our old Shaare Torah had become a church. They suddenly looked embarrassed, and muttered something like "yes?" I then asked Mom if she knew that her old Kesser Torah had also become a church, and she looked more uncomfortable. "Did you know and just not tell me?" I followed up. And sadly, they did know but not reveal this to me. (They also admitted that they did not think I would be concerned.)

Other people view the topic with a sense of distance, and have more of an intellectual curiosity about it. This is what I have often noticed amongst non-Jews who are interested in my work. They see it in terms of urban history and development, architecture, photographic opportunities and related subjects. And I have certainly met many non-Jewish people who want to learn more about these buildings, who have joined my tours, who have some connection to a few of the sites because they may have attended a bar mitzvah or wedding at a particular shul.

One time when I led my East Village walking tour in Manhattan, there were two Swedish architecture students, studying at New York University, who came along on my tour particularly because they were interested in architectural history and wanted to learn more about NYC in general. I was surprised that they would find my tour enlightening but they were enthusiastic about it. And I have met several Christian people from the Bronx, who are very interested in discussing the Bronx former synagogues, because they knew about them as they grew up. They even invited me to speak (once in person and once virtually) at meetings of the East Bronx History Forum.

The number of extant former synagogues, or lost synagogues, can vary over time when certain ones are demolished or others somehow are turned once again into synagogues or other Jewish institutions such as schools, museums or organizations. The former situation is more common than the latter. But the latter has been known to happen too.

Which synagogue and institutional buildings, if any, should be retained and repurposed by the Jewish community? How is this determined? While cities and towns do have landmarking committees and preservation societies, the process is laborious and does not satisfy everyone.

Where will the funding come from? Should we repurpose elements of an old synagogue into a new one (aside from Torah scrolls)?

New synagogues *are* being built in various parts of the United States, from Brooklyn to Florida and elsewhere. This happens even though synagogue buildings in other parts of the US are turned into churches, stores, private homes or warehouses. (Even within Brooklyn, there are new shuls built while others are closed or even torn down.) My role is to make you aware of the former shuls, the so-called lost synagogues, and educate you about their stories and their roles in communities. Once I spoke at a community board meeting in Manhattan when asked to do so by neighborhood residents, to challenge the demolition of a particular active synagogue whose building was around 90 years old. My testimony was applauded, but the building was knocked down later on anyway.

# Some Uncomfortable Truths About Former Synagogues

Religious congregations build synagogues for many reasons. Their members want buildings in which to pray, to gather for religious rituals, to celebrate lifecycle events, to provide classroom space for schools, especially for their children but also for adult education courses, lectures and sessions. They might want to hold cantorial concerts, choir performances or other musical events. They might hope to construct an impressive edifice with which to showcase their rabbi, their cantor, or other dignitaries.

The people within the congregations typically have aspirations for the synagogue buildings they fund and build. Usually they want these buildings to be appealing to their members and also to attract potential additional members. They may want to show themselves to be exemplary pillars of Judaism's tenets. They want to provide a space that is welcoming to their people and perhaps to others as well, within the community and beyond.

Many people also want to take pride in the buildings and the campuses, the lawns and outdoor spaces. They may cherish the decorative elements inside and outside of the buildings, from stained glass windows to grand doors and entrances, from manicured lawns to stately domes, and much more. Even the lawns and gardens of larger synagogues may be well manicured, dotted with artworks or dedication benches and other items. They want attractive settings for assembling the annual sukkahs for the holiday of Sukkot, and perhaps outdoor spaces for public menorah lighting each Hanukkah. They might build playgrounds for their children.

Members of congregations will also look to their houses of worship as depositories of memories. This is why so many synagogues have memorial plaques, pews with metal name tags, beautiful windows with dedications, and other decorative items that incorporate names of people, past and present, who mean something to the congregants and to the congregations. Just as families can be "house proud," congregations can be "synagogue proud," and they want facilities they can show off to themselves and to society.

Then again, this has been true for many congregations but not all. Traveling around the United States, locating and documenting former synagogues as well as active ones, I have seen synagogue buildings that run the gamut of splendor and effort. I've seen large and elaborate buildings, moderate specimens, and rather modest ones as well. Some congregations hired architects of renown to design new structures, while others made minor renovations to existing buildings. Did the congregations responsible for modest synagogue buildings assume that their congregants would move on within a matter of years? Did the fancier synagogue builders expect their sites to last for several generations? Are these decisions always based upon at-hand financial resources, or also seen as long-term investments?

Budgets, fundraising, expectations, dreams and goals: all become part of the synagogue building experience. Sometimes I have wondered why certain congregations invested so much money, space, effort and non-tangibles into buildings that only served as synagogues for twenty to thirty years. Surely, these people may not have anticipated such short tenancies. But they occurred in several places, especially in urban areas. Other tenancies lasted for perhaps five, six, ten or more decades. Yes, there are synagogues I have documented that only lasted for twenty or thirty-odd years, before they morphed into other uses, while others lasted as synagogues for well over a hundred or more years before succumbing to changes.

Also: why did so many congregations build elaborate or at least sizable buildings within close proximity of each other? Weren't they aware of the competition? Were they so sure of their investments? And do I sound cynical? I am. Look at Detroit, and Cleveland, Philadelphia and the Bronx, Chicago and Baltimore, and you will see areas where there are multiple former synagogues. They are often within blocks of each other, or even on the very same block. So many built near each other: how could they be sustainable? Was this a manifestation of irrational exuberance? How could these groups expect so many synagogues, erected so closely to each other, to attract adequate amounts of people? And survive for generations to come?

Or am I looking at these communities with the help of hindsight? My father was a structural engineer, and his childhood was rooted in the Great Depression; both these factors shaped his worldview greatly. In his more skeptical moments he would gaze upon a large building and wisecrack,

"That's a monument to the architect." Extrapolating from this, I often look at large former synagogues and wonder, "Were these monuments to someone?"

The expression "McMansion" originated in the 1980s, and it was used wryly to describe oversized houses meant to dazzle. But the essence of the McMansion surely is much older.

Just as people have so often "dressed to impress" in their choice of clothing, accessories, and bearing, buildings have long been built to impress. But I have seen so many impressive former synagogues, and I put the emphasis on *former*, in a wistful manner.

Large and even not so large synagogue buildings can face a myriad of challenges: unfilled or barely filled pews; general upkeep and maintenance, ranging from leaky roofs to vandalism, from broken boilers and air conditioners to plumbing problems and warped or cracked stained glass windows; renovations that can be costly, from adding features to accommodate people with disabilities to energy-saving lighting, and much more.

Then there is the vague but foreboding term "changing demographics." Factors include upward mobility; fears of non-Jewish groups; changes in religious fervor; and other trends. While Jews may have felt more comfortable in certain neighborhoods, for the most part they were not restricted from being mobile. Like many other people in the United States over time, if they had the desire and the means to move, they decamped (with varying degrees of willingness). The European ghettos and restricted Jewish areas of Middle Eastern and North African communities were a thing of the past for American Jews.

Even if there was covert discrimination and certain areas were off limits, so many other areas were available, and this impacted synagogue membership. A particular urban synagogue may have drawn congregants from 1920 through the mid-1960s,but then members may have moved en masse, while others died, and those remaining may not have had the means or desire to keep a particular congregation going. It's reality, and it can be viewed as a sad reality, or positive, or in a more nuanced way.

Have we failed by leaving all these buildings? I don't think so, but we should grapple with this. I have heard from some Jews who regard lost synagogues as our failures to sustain the Jewish community in a fitting manner. These people often discern all these buildings, turned into churches or medical centers and such, and see the Jewish community's (or communities) failure to keep "Jews in the pews." They may bemoan this, or even experience anger, view the younger generations as irresponsible, lazy, uncommitted. But this does not explain fully why there are so many former shuls. In small towns the former synagogues may have been left by people who went to larger regions with better economic opportunities. In urban neighborhoods the people may have gravitated toward suburbs, or to more desirable precincts. A group may have felt that its earlier building did not suit its growing or evolving needs. And this has happened not only to synagogues, but also to church congregations throughout the United States that have shrunk or even closed.

I admit that I do not have all the answers as to why particular synagogue buildings have closed. Sometimes they are obvious, other times they are hard to discern. One shul may have closed a building in order to move to a bigger one. Or the congregants made it clear that they did not feel safe any longer in their neighborhood and were moving away. Yes, in many cases there was fear, prejudice, mistrust, misunderstanding of "others" that burgeoned into what is often referred to as "white flight" (and this assumes that the majority of Jews have been considered "white," even if there are many Jews of color).

There are also uncomfortable truths about how a synagogue becomes "decommissioned". Usually I visit these buildings when they have stopped serving the Jewish populace, sometimes a few generations earlier. But I have observed a few that were in the process of closing. There are at least three synagogues in Brooklyn that I watched in their sunset years, which were closed and remade. One in Bensonhurst, Brooklyn I watched up close for a few years, because a family friend had been a congregant. Another in Canarsie, Brooklyn I knew less about but still had been aware of it for over twenty years (I would pass it as I drove by or took buses). And one former synagogue in the Prospect Heights section of Brooklyn, which I had seen as a church, had been abandoned and then I watched it on the first day of demolition, videotaping and photographing the interior and exterior over several months.

Another synagogue, a legendary congregation on the Lower East Side, was felled by a hurricane and then by arson, so I watched it being dismantled and scrapped. (And now a modern high rise has taken its place.)

When a synagogue is in its final days, the congregants and clergy may follow closing rituals to decommission the building in a proper Jewish manner. They may take all the Torah scrolls and march them around in circuits or *hakafot*, as a means of bidding farewell in a formal way.

They may march with the scrolls to a new building, or pack them up and have them shipped to some place far away, that promises to honor the memory of this closing shul. In one case, I found an archived flier with the mapped-out route, for a Detroit congregation that was moving from one building to a newer one in another neighborhood. They marched with the Torahs.

Another way that congregations may close out formally is in meetings where any remaining assets are divided up. These items could include money, cemetery plots, prayer books, small memorial plaques, even stained glass windows and other decorative elements. Sometimes the congregations have done this with legal assistance, but at other times the groups really did abandon the buildings.

In many cases there are real estate dealings that occur in tandem with the decommissioning activities. At times the synagogue boards have outright sold the buildings to other religious groups, but in many situations the boards instead sold their synagogue buildings to an agent, who then flipped the property to another religious group. (This "flipping" was often seen as less odious and embarrassing, and more in keeping with religious customs and laws.)

In many cases the decommissioning also involved finding homes (such as other synagogues and schools, or libraries and archives) for items such as Torah scrolls, prayer books, memorial plaque boards, even ephemera such as Membership roll books, archival items, collections of bulletins and more. I have encountered archival holdings at libraries and archives, occasionally elsewhere, for some congregations because a savvy member or clergy person thought to bring these items for posterity to a place such as Yeshiva University, the Jewish Theological Seminary, the New York Public Library, or even college archives.

In general, the decommissioning and leave taking of synagogues has not been a happy subject. It is painful, disappointing, embarrassing, mournful and so on. It is discomforting, and something I often wonder about because for the most part, it has not been well documented. Saying farewell to a synagogue because it has essentially died out, is sad. I visit these buildings years, even decades after they closed, and rarely did these places document the bitter ends because they were so sad. (I can think of a synagogue within New York City that is for all intents and purposes unused, but a few holdout members are refusing to close it down officially.)

But for my purposes, I have appreciated visiting those buildings which remain, even if they were later turned into churches, or mosques, or Hindu temples, or medical centers, or private homes, and so on. At least they still stand, unlike the many that have been torn down. (And just because I got to visit a particular former synagogue in 2006, and then several other times, does not mean it will not be torn down later.)

I have dealt with people who are angry at the conditions of some lost synagogues, and blame the current inhabitants. But the groups that move in do not always have the funds to fix up the crumbling details and main sanctuaries. I have dealt with other people who develop resentments toward the churches and other inheritors. In a few cases people have suggested what I consider rather far-fetched ideas: why couldn't these synagogue buildings be moved elsewhere? (This is so difficult, rarely feasible.) Why couldn't this synagogue building have been turned into a museum? (Do you want to undertake this task? It is difficult and costly to do.) There are a handful, including the Lloyd Street synagogue in Baltimore and the Eldridge Street Synagogue in Manhattan. But we cannot turn every closed shul into a museum.

I have dealt with people who espouse conspiracies and flat-out denial. In the early years of my documenting the lost synagogues on Facebook, a woman kept commenting that I was lying; synagogues could not have become churches! She asked why I was lying so blatantly. I would try to be as patient as possible, and write explanations, and assert that I was not lying about the status of former synagogues. After a while I had to block her from my page because her harangues became a source of absurd pestering. She disliked the reality I was documenting.

More commonly, I encountered people who did not like my "airing dirty laundry" about Jewish communities and synagogues that had been closed. That makes more sense but I also felt that these people were denying historical changes and that was not good either. Things happen and just because they make you uncomfortable, does not mean they should not be examined. History is not always pretty; it has plenty of painful and irksome episodes, to put it mildly.

So yes, my many years of researching, visiting, photographing and analyzing former synagogues have not always been easy, nor cheerful. But there is so much to be learned, to be made available to people who want to learn about the subject and related topics such as architecture, genealogy, geography, and so on.

I thought even more about the impact and intersection of home buying costs, synagogues, and related trends when I came across a Facebook discussion in the group "Serious Discourse About Conservative Judaism" (found online at https://www.facebook.com/groups/2225630921006309/).

The back and forth about high housing costs in neighborhoods that had shuls within walking distance caused me to think about how so many synagogues, in suburban as well as urban areas, were built so close to each other due to walkability, but when congregants moved away (for their various reasons) there were so many buildings left empty. In addition, especially in suburban areas, there were synagogue buildings constructed with parking lots with the assumption that congregants would drive there. Yet many of these buildings also closed down. Driveability and a parking lot could not stave off the closures of certain urban and suburban synagogues.

I have visited urban neighborhoods that have experienced a revival (or you might classify it as "gentrification") where Jews have moved back, such as the Lower East Side and East Village, Harlem, Bed-Stuy and Flatbush in New York City. I also saw this in parts of Philadelphia and Detroit. But just because Jews have returned does not mean all the former synagogues that became churches will suddenly flip back to being synagogues. I know of one Brooklyn Jewish school, that later became a secular preschool, and later was turned into a yeshiva, but this is a rarity. More often, the Jews that come back to these neighborhoods will establish new congregations or travel to other neighborhoods and attend synagogues there.

Other factors have been at work in the process of how synagogue buildings change, among them Orthodox versus non-Orthodox congregations, urban versus suburban, or (once) outlier areas that become majority areas. In many cities such as New York, Newark, Detroit, Pittsburgh, Cleveland, most of the synagogues that closed were Orthodox and traditional. But in some of the suburbs, such as Long Island, you see more Reform and Conservative shuls that closed. And I have documented Conservative and Reform synagogues in New York City, Chicago, and elsewhere that also closed.

One day I spoke on the phone with Sergey Kadinsky, who mentioned to me that some people just don't want to live near their parents, so they move away and establish synagogues elsewhere. Certainly this also contributes to the closure of many synagogues, this sense of what could be cutting the apron strings, or striving, or even wanderlust. And I would be remiss if I did not mention that some lost or almost lost synagogues have been bought later on by and turned into Chabad congregations, or remade into *yeshivot* (religious schools) in Canarsie and some parts of Queens.

Finally, another uncomfortable factor in my research, which pointed out how my thinking had been rather insular for too long, was going beyond my "New York-centric lens" or bias, in order to see how the former synagogue situations elsewhere in the US are not just similar to that of New York City and Long Island, but unique to those areas. Especially by visiting parts of the midwest and upstate New York, the Mid-Atlantic and New England, I pushed myself to see how not every synagogue is a variation on New York prototypes. Even visiting Philadelphia, Newark and Jersey City more than once (and in multiple years), and revisiting Cleveland and San Francisco, helped me to better understand the factors within these cities.

I realized that I had taken liberties by making so many comparisons (and assumptions) about Jewish communities beyond New York City and Long Island, and I needed to learn more and document better the synagogues in many other parts of the US. Although I have not (yet) visited every region of the US and every single former synagogue building, I have gained a much greater understanding of the way synagogues have been built, how communities changed over time, and how some cities have undergone greater upheaval than others. So many factors have been involved. These stories are not neatly compartmentalized. There are general trends and individual stories.

# The Past, Present and Future For Former Synagogues: In Brief

On Sunday, November 2, 2025 I attended "The Past, Present, and Future of Jewish History," a symposium at the Center for Jewish History in Manhattan. Intriguing panel discussions were offered, with academics from various colleges analyzing aspects of this topic.

I found it very interesting, and focused my attention on two panels: "How Significant is Antisemitism in Jewish History?" and "Who Counts in Jewish History?"

I reflected on how these two discussions may have shaped my field of research on lost synagogues and their documentation. In keeping with the style of overarching questions (after all, I taught high school social studies for many years), I will pose questions and give basic answers, by no means comprehensive and final.

1. Has antisemitism influenced my work on Former Synagogues?

Antisemitism has long been a problem for society, lurking in the background at times, and frequently in the news these past few years. Perhaps it has influenced my work, although it did not prompt my work at the start, nor has it been the overriding factor. Have I felt it important to showcase Jewish history, and is my work part of Jewish history? Yes, both indeed. And sadly, on a few occasions people have made antisemitic remarks on social media about my work, on particular posts. But overall, I don't think it has been a major influence.

2. How has antisemitism impacted the closing of synagogues and other Jewish institutions?

In individual cases, it could have been a factor. I think in the Bronx in particular, this may have been a factor in the brutal treatment of some synagogue buildings that fell victim to vandalism and arson. (However, that happened to many other non-Jewish buildings in the Bronx and was a product of the general wretched conditions and trends in the Bronx at that time.) And perhaps it impacted other parts of the US with which I have less familiarity; I am thinking of Newark, New Jersey and elsewhere. But in general, many other factors have held a bigger role: shifting demographics due to mobility, consideration of "moving up" into "better" areas, consolidation of congregations, changes in observance levels and synagogue attendance, general assimilation for many Jewish people, and more.

3. Has the shifting population density of Jewish areas, especially in urban America, been impacted by antisemitism– as opposed to economic, class, intergroup relations, etc?

This is hard to say. Yes, there have been many incidents of Jewish people in urban America who were bullied over time, in overt and covert ways, and that may have prompted some Jews to move out of certain neighborhoods. But I think that in many cases, other factors have been intertwined: economic concerns, class status, assertion over turf, various ethnicities squabbling with each other and also cooperating, and so on.

For example, did antisemitism cause Jews in Brownsville to leave for other parts of Brooklyn, or suburbs, or Florida? I think this could be a stretch, unless you ignore upward mobility, the building of large public housing projects, etc.

4. Did shuls with obvious and even ostentatious Judaica show stronger Jewish pride?

I have wondered about this. To some extent yes, but it is also a factor of finances. Bigger shul buildings usually reflected bigger endowments and/or wealthier benefactors, greater fundraising, and so on. This also reflected the individual tastes of building committees, of artisans hired along the way, even of inherited tastes. For example, some synagogues decorated the interiors of their buildings (especially foyers and sanctuaries) with particular murals and symbols, even painting ceilings to resemble the sky/heaven, to reflect artistic styles from "the old country." That is not so much showing off as preserving styles, or recreating customs.

5. What is the future of Former Synagogues?

I assume that more synagogues will close. But new synagogues will open. Some will consolidate and merge with each other. Some will shutter their doors with no clear continuation, especially in small towns and rural areas but also in cities. Will people continue to document their histories? I hope so. I hope dearly that my work will continue to inspire other people to create new archives and add to existing ones, and perhaps write more books, or at least articles and essays. I do hope my work will continue to be of scholarly importance. (There was discussion of archives in the panel on "Who Counts?") Professor Alanna E. Cooper has noted that there are 20% fewer synagogues active today than in 1990. At this point in time, more synagogues in the US are closing each year than are opening. So there will be an increase in former synagogues, sad to say. A further question should be, how will the decreasing number of synagogues impact Jews? And, how will knowledge about former synagogues impact American Jews?

6. Is this book (and the previous lost synagogues trilogy) strictly Jewish studies?

I don't think so. I have long contended that my work in this field can be of interest to many people: those interested in urban history and also suburban; religious studies in general; architecture students and fans; those interested in genealogy; and more. I have often been surprised by the interest shown by and the inquiries made by non-Jewish folks curious about the buildings in general and sometimes particular sites. However, I have spoken with at least two professors who told me that they referenced my earlier books in one or more of their courses, and both these professors taught Jewish studies.

7. What are the hard questions for my topic?

Why should people care about buildings that were synagogues but no longer function as such?

What happens when a former synagogue is demolished or destroyed in another manner?

Isn't a former synagogue an embarrassment? Why should I promote the study of these if they are an embarrassment, or an admission of Jewish people being unable or uninterested in maintaining their houses of worship and other institutions?

8. How do former synagogues count in US Jewish history?

These sources certainly do count: the shul buildings themselves, the memorial plaques, archival items, memories. Interviews, memorabilia such as photographs, ritual items, high holiday tickets, congregational bulletins (weekly, monthly, bimonthly), Golden books, accounting ledgers, and so much more.

Aside from the tangible items, former synagogues count because they were sites for prayer, for holidays as well as weekly and even daily prayer groups, for life-cycle events such as bar/ bat mitzvah ceremonies, weddings, funerals. They were sites for fundraising activities and community meetings. Schools (especially supplemental but also day schools, and also adult education) met in their rooms and sanctuaries. Choirs performed and lecturers spoke in these buildings. Sometimes politicians and civic leaders spoke here too.

Although not every Jewish person has attended synagogues regularly, many have at some points in their lives, at least occasionally. Synagogues are viewed as extremely important to Jewish communal life. Non-Jews sometimes attend as well, as guests or out of curiosity. These reasons are why former synagogues COUNT.

9. How might AI impact the study of former synagogues?

People might not believe that a particular building actually functioned as a synagogue in the past. They might see a doctored or fake image of a former synagogue and that can mislead them. Particular former synagogues could be misrepresented in size, design, condition, decorative elements, etc. The information about the congregations could be inaccurate. I am very wary of AI in general, as far as photography, writing, archival upkeep, and other reasons.

There are other "hard questions" to ask about former synagogues. Please ask them and conduct more research.

# Looking at Jewish Population Numbers in the United States

The areas of greater Jewish population within the United States have supported a larger number of synagogues, schools and other Jewish institutions. In general, I have also found more *former* synagogues, schools and other Jewish institutions in these areas. New York City, Philadelphia and Chicago are three of the most prominent examples. Overall, urban areas (and nearby suburbs) have been home to a greater number of such sites. For example, Long Island, a large area that is a primary suburb of New York City, does have many active as well as former synagogues and related buildings.

One might assume that a sizable Jewish population would lead to a large number of synagogues and perhaps a large number of *former* synagogues, for a variety of reasons. But there are several factors at work here. Keep in mind that while some parts of the US have had consistently significant Jewish populations (such as NYC), others have seen considerable fluctuations.

One example of the latter would be Newark, New Jersey. For several generations Newark had a notable Jewish population and many synagogues, but after the 1960s that number dropped considerably. Whereas Newark had over forty shuls in its heyday, as of 2025 it has one mainstream synagogue (Ahavas Sholom), a Chabad congregation, and a tiny number of Black Hebrew congregations. Decades ago, some mainstream Newark congregations relocated to nearby suburbs.

Even within the few American cities with consistently large Jewish populations, there have been shifts of residential concentration. For instance, Brooklyn has had a large Jewish population since the early 1900s, but Jews have moved around to a certain degree. Brownsville and Canarsie had many more Jews before the 1970s and now have very few; Park Slope and nearby Windsor Terrace have more. This has led to a number of former synagogues in Brownsville and Canarsie, but more active ones in Park Slope (and also nearby Prospect Heights). There have been comparable shifts within Philadelphia and Chicago.

Certainly in recent decades the United States has had one of the largest populations of Jews in the world. According to World Population Review, in 2023 the US did indeed hold the top spot. In the recent past Israel had more[1]. But the US was not always the first or even the second largest center of Jewish life; from the 1880s through the early 1920s the Jewish population of the US increased monumentally due largely to migration from Europe and to a lesser extent other regions.

The US Library of Congress, in the web article "A Century of Immigration, 1820–1924"

A Century of Immigration, 1820–1924—From Haven to Home: 350 Years of Jewish Life in America | Exhibitions (Library of Congress) states that

> "In the first half of the nineteenth century, Jewish immigrants came mostly, though not exclusively, from Central Europe. In addition to settling in New York, Philadelphia, and Baltimore, groups of German-speaking Jews made their way to Cincinnati, Albany, Cleveland, Louisville, Minneapolis, St. Louis, New Orleans, San Francisco, and dozens of small towns across the United States. During this period there was an almost hundred-fold increase in America's Jewish population from some 3,000 in 1820 to as many as 300,000 in 1880."[2]

According to Wikipedia, in the article "Jewish population by city," the American cities in 2021 with the largest populations were:

*New York City–2,109,300*

Los Angeles–622,480

Miami–535,500

*Philadelphia–419,850*

Washington, DC–297,290

*Chicago–294,280*

Boston–257,460

1. https://worldpopulationreview.com/country-rankings/jewish-population-by-country.

2. https://www.loc.gov/exhibits/haventohome/haven-century.html

*San Francisco–244,000*

Atlanta–119,800

*Baltimore–117,800*

San Diego–100,000[3]

I have documented former synagogues in the italicized cities. While that does not necessarily equal the largest number of former synagogues for each city, my studies have shown that the largest numbers of former synagogues have been in NYC (undeniably first place), Philadelphia, Chicago and Baltimore all with several. (SF only has a tiny number.) Detroit (number thirty six) and Cleveland (number thirty) have many former synagogues but in 2021 their Jewish populations were not nearly as large. Other cities that I have documented here such as Buffalo, Syracuse and Albany in New York, New Orleans, and Toledo (Ohio) have much smaller Jewish populations as of 2021.Thus, the original assumption about populations leading to a number of former synagogues is not always valid.

Going back earlier, to 1948, we can see some interesting precursors to this ranking of population. According to data derived from the American Jewish Year Book, these were the totals for Jewish populations in American places that I documented:

*Connecticut:*

Bridgeport: 11,550

Hartford: 26,000

Meriden: 1,200

New Haven: 20,000

Chicago: 300,000

New Orleans: 7,500

Baltimore: 75,000

Detroit: 90,000

3. https://en.wikipedia.org/wiki/Jewish_population_by_city

*New Jersey:*

Bayonne: 12,000

Camden: 6,517

Jersey City: 18,000

Newark: 56,800

Passaic & Clifton: 12,000

Paterson: 20,000

Perth Amboy: 4,500

*New York:*

Albany: 9,000

Buffalo: 19,600

Kingston: 2,400

Mount Vernon: 10,000

Newburgh: 2,200

NYC: 2,000,000

Poughkeepsie: 2,500

Rochester: 20,000

Schenectady: 3,725

Syracuse: 10,000

White Plains: 3,000

Yonkers: 6,750

*Ohio:*

Cleveland: 80,000

Toledo: 6,500

*Pennsylvania:*

Erie: 1,750

Philadelphia: 245,000

Pittsburgh: 54,000

Reading: 3,000

These numbers are certainly important and informative, but they do not necessarily correlate to the number of former synagogues still standing in the early 2000s. As I have learned through research, including reading and studying maps, there are many former synagogues that have been *demolished.* They are truly gone.

The fact that former synagogues have been torn down is a game changer in my research; it means these are buildings, even campuses, that can no longer be visited in person. They may have left a presence in other ways (online, in museum collections, via religious items and plaques redistributed to other active synagogues and schools) but I am not focusing on them because they are gone and cannot be seen in person.

The largest number of former synagogues that I have documented is in New York City, and the second largest is in Chicago. But when I searched for many other lost shuls, given the addresses I gleaned, I realized that many others are simply gone. Synagogue buildings can be torn down for various reasons (their state of decrepitude and even collapse, the desire for that plot of land, arson, eminent domain for public use, and so on).

Thus, by choosing to document synagogue and Jewish institutional buildings that still stand (and sadly, a few have been torn down even since my visits), my documentation numbers have been impacted. Also, some cities have not had as many synagogues opened and closed, so that impacted the number. It is not surprising, for example, that a city such as Detroit has a significant number of lost synagogue buildings because the Jewish population dwindled greatly in the actual city. (And some of the buildings were also torn down due to their condition.) But the story in New York City is different because while this is still the American city with the largest Jewish population, it has had many synagogue buildings closed in some areas, but more built in other neighborhoods.

# Travels: Curtailed (Then Resumed)

To research former synagogues, and do a respectable job of it, you need to invest a lot of time into the work. I became serious about this subject in the early 2000s, initially as a photography project. Every year since 2003 or so, I have probably spent at least the equivalent of one to two months' time, visiting and revisiting former synagogues throughout NYC and elsewhere. I have done this willingly, but still, it is an investment of time.

Some former synagogues I visited while on vacation (San Francisco, New Orleans, the first trip to Cleveland) but many of the excursions were specifically (or mostly) geared toward documenting these sites. Even with Covid-19 lurking in the background, since 2020 I have managed to visit several parts of New Jersey, and many sections of New York State (and re-visited many of the NYC lost synagogues I had documented in my earlier books). I also racked up miles driving to Connecticut, Philadelphia and nearby areas, Baltimore (twice), Ohio (Cleveland the second time) and Michigan. The last major trip I undertook was to Chicago; that two-day trip amounted to a race for me, to see how many former synagogues I could visit before it grew dark (Day One) and before I headed back to the airport (Day Two). In addition I took shorter trips to Long Island, Westchester and Rockland, all within an hour or two from my home.

What *did* curtail my travel and documentation of former synagogues was breaking my right femur, during a bad slip and fall on the front steps of my house. This happened in mid-April 2024. I had plans to visit a few other cities before my severely broken leg and major surgery, but they were postponed. In retrospect I had nearly enough sites visited, but I also had to stop researching and writing for a while.

Regaining my ability to drive brought back my mobility, and access to my laptop allowed me to do the online research and writing chores. But while I was recuperating at a local rehabilitation facility, I reflected on the fact that driving was an integral part of my documentation of lost synagogues. Although I have visited some local examples by taking public transportation within New York City (especially Brooklyn, Manhattan and the Bronx), I have visited the vast majority of synagogues, especially for this book, via car trips.

Ironically, many congregants of the old synagogues walked to their synagogues and eschewed both cars and public transit. This was particularly true of urban synagogues, less so of suburban and small-town synagogues (several of which even provided parking lots for congregants).

Being unable to drive for over two months gave me time to think carefully about the many former shuls I had visited, scrutinizing the photographs and notes I had taken over the years.

Although I have not managed to visit every single lost synagogue, nor every city and town with former shuls, I did see a large swath of them. It definitely helped that I was willing and able to do extensive driving as well as using public transportation in certain areas. Hopefully my former synagogue travels will not be curtailed again.

# More Former Synagogues in Brooklyn

I HAVE ALREADY WRITTEN three books about former synagogues throughout New York City, all published by Avotaynu: The Lost Synagogues of Brooklyn (2009), The Lost Synagogues of the Bronx and Queens (2011) and The Lost Synagogues of Manhattan (2013); the third title in the trilogy also included Staten Island and Governors Island. None have been updated with newer editions. However, several synagogues and Jewish schools in New York City have closed since then. In addition, there were older ones that I just did not find previously. I will begin with Brooklyn, because that was my original starting place. From there I will cover the Bronx and Queens.

My book The Lost Synagogues of Brooklyn was published in 2009, and since then there have been more synagogues in Kings County that have closed. In a few cases they moved, or merged with another group. In addition, I missed documenting other synagogues and Jewish institutions and am now including them in this book. These sites are found in several neighborhoods, and a few are what I would classify as "outliers" because either there were few synagogues in those areas, or they are located just outside of neighborhoods that are heavily or at least moderately populated by Jews.

Property data is also included from the NYC Department of Finance website. New York City easily makes such information available online.

*B'nai Israel*
*5322 4th Avenue | 11220*
Regular | NW corner | Building 50x100 | 1 story

This corner building is an example of a former synagogue that has been a church longer than it was ever a Jewish house of worship. Yes, there are remaining bits of Judaica even today, such as a cornerstone that reads "5618/1917" in a wavy, atypical font. There are stained glass windows from the days of the synagogue, but various details have been altered by one or both of the churches that have been here for many years. In the 1939–40 Tax photo, this synagogue had a Jewish star atop the roofline, over the main entrance. A sign read "Salem" in English. Thus the Jewish congregation only spent about two decades in this building before it became a church. (Salem apparently purchased the B'nai Israel building for $60,000.) Later on it became the Sunset Park Community Church.This has not been a heavily Jewish area overall; I would classify this short-lived congregation as having an outlier status.

*Temple Beth El*
*1656 West 10th Street | 11223*
Regular | Building 50x88 | 2 stories | Masonry | Built 1908

This building was originally a church, and became a synagogue later on. According to the American Synagogue Directory of 1960 they were led by Rabbi Harry M. Katzen and their president was William Turner. Our family friend who had belonged to the synagogue for many years, Charles E., tipped me off to the forthcoming closure. The congregation had made sure in advance that memorial plaques were transferred to another Brooklyn synagogue.

I attended a Shabbat service there one time, and later on visited perhaps a year before it closed for good. The synagogue president showed me around the facility and let me take mementoes. Among the pieces of memorabilia I took were pieces of stationery with the letterhead, a youth group photo in black-and-white, and a High Holidays ticket. Nothing extraordinary, but typical items used at a contemporary American synagogue. The building was a mix of early 20th Century construction with mid-century decor in faded colors. There were a few stained glass windows, and at least two had noticeable cracks. But now these are gone. An Asian-American community group took over the building, and removed the Judaica. The one item that remains is the "1901" cornerstone; yet this structure is listed as having been built in 1908. Curious.

*The Jewish Hospital*
*555 (545) Prospect Place | 11238*
Building 200x72 | Masonry | 12 stories

This is a large, stately facility and you can still see the name in English, on the Prospect Place side, above the main entrance. The western side is on Classon Avenue and the campus extends between Prospect Place and St. Marks Avenue, a full block. This sizable facility opened in 1906, and included a nursing school. The architect George Morse worked on the main building. The Jonas family has been memorialized in a few spots on the exterior of the building complex; Nathan Jonas donated land for the campus. According to the American Synagogue Directory of 1960 they had a rabbi on the premises, R. Harry Katzen and the president was Isidor Leviton.

It ceased to function as a hospital when it merged with St. John's Episcopal Hospital in 1983 and a new hospital was built in another Brooklyn neighborhood, known as Interfaith Medical Center.

The synagogue Temple Isaac was located across the street on Prospect Place, but that building became a church and was later vacant. It was demolished by 2019. (I wrote about this sad ending in an article for the website *Brownstoner.*) In May 2024 the complex made the local news when a fire broke out in one apartment. A cousin of mine lives in an apartment here and likes the design.

*East Midwood Hebrew Day School/Rabbi Harry Halpern Day School*
*1256 East 21st | 11210*
Regular | Building 166x63 | 3 stories | Masonry

I knew this building well, because I spent a considerable amount of my school years here, in the after-school Talmud Torah/Hebrew school program. From second through twelfth grades, I attended classes on weekdays and Sundays here. My own daughters attended the Day School for their early years of schooling. I also went here for youth activities such as Junior Congregation (Saturday morning and holiday services) and for Young Judaea youth group meetings, and occasional other activities and events. A few hundred children each year, in its busiest years, attended Day School and Hebrew school classes in this building.

The Day School was founded in 1956 and the name changed a few times. For more than three decades the Educational Director was Dr. Aryeh Rohn. Mrs. Jennie Brooks was the Hebrew High School principal for many years. The Hebrew School began in this building in 1949; a cornerstone gives the Hebrew date as well and refers to it as the "religious school." A much larger engraved sign is seen over the entrance to the school. The font used for this is unusual and striking. It was closed in 2018. For one year another Jewish day school was located here, and then in 2020, a charter high school called Urban Dove moved into the building after a major interior renovation. The building's exterior still features various exterior elements from the Jewish school days. There are two gray cornerstones, and a large carved stone sign (in an interesting font) that features the Talmud Torah name and a Jewish star.

*United Sephardim of Brooklyn*
*699 Williams Avenue | 11207*
Irregular | Building 112x58.75 | 2 stories | Built 1930

The origin story of this building is not typical of other former synagogues throughout Brooklyn. This site on Williams was one of three Sephardic synagogues in the New Lots neighborhood, all linked by ethnic association. This one was the Monastirlis Society synagogue; it was also the site of several bar mitzvah ceremonies for the association. One of the "brother" synagogues was located on Hinsdale Street, and the third on nearby Malta Street. (I documented those two in my previous Brooklyn book.) There does not appear to be any remaining Judaica outside, nor inside (based upon the one time I was inside, around 2015 or 2016). In the American Synagogue Directory of 1960 the rabbi listed was Arnold B. Marans and their president was Jack Wohl. The community later moved away, with some members going to nearby Canarsie for a few decades, others to Queens and Nassau County, while others moved to other parts of Brooklyn such as Gravesend, Mill Basin and Midwood. The building itself is not unusual (it is basically a rectangle) but the fact that it stands by itself on a short triangular block, bordered by two others (Williams and Louisiana Avenues on the longer sides, Hegeman Avenue on the short southern edge) makes it atypical.

*Darchei-Zedek Jewish Community Center*
*969 Hegeman Avenue | 11208*
Building 15x60 | 1 story | Stone | Built 1929

Some former synagogues are a mere single story in height, such as this building that has functioned as a residential property for decades. In the 1939–40 Tax photo, this address was home to a synagogue and there were at least two Jewish stars in windows, one each above doorways. It was a fairly unadorned building aside from that, then and even now as a private residence. In fact, now the remaining Judaica is only obvious on the

Berriman Street side of the building. The American Synagogue Directory of 1960 informs us that they were led by Rabbi R. Michael Scholar and the president was Jack Brodsky. But apparently the congregation closed down by the late 1960s, according to Steve Stein on a JewishGen discussion board.

*Beth Aaron Synagogue*
*2261 Bragg Street | 11229*
Irregular | Building 59x90 | 2 stories | Masonry | Built 1953

This former synagogue, a post World War 2 construction, has sat vacant since 2000. According to a New York Post article dated September 1, 2000, "Brooklyn Synagogue Fire Devastates Worshippers," a fire greatly damaged the synagogue. Two rabbis, both brothers, had been leading this congregation since the late 1980s. Its fate has been debated for quite some time, and in 2016 the Forward published an article about how there were supposed plans to turn the site into a halfway house. But that has been on ice, and the building just grows more woebegone. And there is still Judaica visible on the exterior, the shul name, two cornerstones, and a seven-branched menorah design. The cornerstone on the far right front reads "In Memory of Benjamin Ellman."

*Chevrah Ain Yacoff Anshai Brownsville*
*1905 Sterling Place | 11233*
Irregular | Building 33x55 | 3 stories | Masonry | Built 1921

Some former synagogues feature only one or two pieces of Judaica that identify their past. This is one such site, where the only obvious Jewish detail is a Magen David star of ornate metal work, in front of the main entrance of what is now a church. In the 1939–40 Tax photo you can see how pretty this building was from the front, even if it was a basic box shape. There was a Jewish star atop a triangle that was at the top of the building. There was a set of beautiful stained glass windows and the center one had a Jewish star. Today there are still a number of nice decorative elements of a general secular nature.

*Congregation Avodas Israel*
*42 Porter Avenue | 11237*
Regular | NW corner | Building 25x70 |
3 stories | Stone | Built 1931

This former synagogue had long been a bit of a mystery to me, and I was unable to find out much about it until two followers of my Facebook page stepped in and did research! Thanks go to Rob Novak and Rick Luftglass, for locating sources in Yiddish newspapers.(Der Morgan Zhurnal) There is a small Jewish star on the bigger part of the building, and the smaller part has a decorative space near the roofline that may have held a sign at some point.

A church resides here now, and the pastor knew no substantive details of the synagogue.

*Ohel Yitzhok*
*1419 Dorchester Road (at Marlborough Road) | 11226*
Regular | NW corner | Building 32x52 |
2 stories | Built 1904

I was inside this building at least twice; once when it was still an active synagogue, and the rabbi showed me items that were saved from other lost Brooklyn synagogues, and again a month or so after it ceased to serve the congregation. Originally built as a church, with a pipe organ, this corner building has an interesting charm. There is a main entrance at the corner, and a secondary one on the Marlborough Road side. You can see Jewish stars from the street in a few windows.

There are several plaques here from the former Prospect Park Jewish Center on Ocean Avenue (now a church) and from Temple Isaac on Prospect Place (which was demolished). Officially the congregation took on the names of Temple Isaac (but translated into Hebrew) and Prospect Park.

When I last visited inside, it was as if time had frozen: there were scattered ritual items and fliers about weekly events, laying around on seats and tables. There was a schedule for the week of February 10, 2022. On the bimah there were two carved wood Lions of Judah, above the Holy Ark doors and below the pipes of the unused organ. I gazed at memorial plaque boards and recognized some of the surnames, including those of the Nachamie family.

There were several pretty stained glass windows with Bible scenes, Jewish stars and other motifs. Rabbi Leib Kelman was the spiritual leader.

Now the building is known as Aleph Early Learning Center, a school for young children, and the connecting building serves as the Dorchester Senior Citizens Center, with a kitchen area.

*Congregation Etz Chaim Anshei Lubin*
*928 DeKalb Avenue | 11221*
Regular | Building 20x50 | 3 stories | Masonry | Built 1931

Sometime between late 2020 and mid-2021, this former synagogue that had served as a church for many years, became a mosque. The building itself is not remarkable, a basic box with some nice brick detailing and a Jewish star at the peak of the roofline. Where there once was a pretty rose window on the second floor is now a plain window of three colors. When I visited inside in the late 2010s, during a Sunday school session, there were some other Jewish remnants inside the balcony. In the 1939–40 Tax photo, this building had a slightly exotic entrance: an ogee atop the main doors, with the name in pretty Hebrew script. The central rose window on the second floor had a Jewish star and several pretty panels. A sign above a first floor window advertised "Heder" or a school. In the 1980s tax photo the entrance had been modified to a plainer design.

According to the American Synagogue Directory of 1960 they were helmed by Rabbi Aron Zlotowitz and the president was Jacob Stock.

*Home for the Aged*
*5810 Snyder Avenue (at East 59th Street) | 11203*
Regular | SW corner | two buildings |
(main one is two stories) | Masonry Built 1935

This former Jewish institution is really a campus: a main building, a much smaller building and a yard, with a prominent fence that features Jewish stars. The main building resembles a school (and is used as such now), a boxy brick structure with some Judaica and historical markers on the front: a central Jewish star below the roofline, an "organized" dedication on the left and another for "dedication" on the right; and a few Jewish stars on the railings.

The sizable open area at the street corner is guarded by several Jewish stars on the fence. The most curious part of this set up is the small building in the back of the yard, with its sign reading "Designed & Erected By Oscar Joroff Sons" and the faded evidence of two Jewish stars that were removed. Was this used as a tiny shul? A social hall?

*Yeshiva Rabbi David Leibowitz*
*9102 Church Ave (at East 91st Street) | 11236*
Regular | SE corner | Building 100x128 |
1 story | Masonry Built 1931

This squat corner building doesn't seem special, until you look closely at the several small Jewish stars that are set just below the roofline. There are also two Jewish stars at the subdued entrance on the East 91st Street side. The building housed a yeshiva, a religious day school, named for a prominent rabbi. When Rabbi Leibowitz came to the United States from Europe, he first taught at Mesivta Torah Vadaath, and later the Yeshiva Chofetz Chaim (also named for a famous rabbi to whom he was related). Both these schools were located elsewhere in Brooklyn. Leibowitz died in 1941.According to the American Synagogue Directory of 1960 they were led by Rabbi Max Tropper and the president was Rabbi A. H. Leibowitz. The school was featured in a New York Times article in 1971 because three "Black Jewish" students were ousted from a Brooklyn yeshiva but then accepted at Yeshiva Rabbi David Leibowitz.

*First Austro-Hungarian Beth Sholom or Bais Aaron Bais Sholem Mikro Kodesh*
*23 Marcus Garvey Boulevard/Sumner Avenue | 11206*
Regular | Building 25x90 | 2 stories | Masonry | Built 1910

This is a row house style former synagogue. It was one of the oldest Orthodox Jewish synagogues purpose-built in Brooklyn.(There are a few Orthodox synagogues that were older but they were built originally as churches.) In the 1940s tax photo you can see the elaborate Jewish star rose window. In the 1980s tax photo the Jewish star design was gone, with a cross in its place. In the American Synagogue Directory it is listed as Bais Aaron, and the rabbi was Ephraim Berman and the president was Ben Zion Lefkowitz

*Beth Abraham*
*301 Sea Breeze Avenue | 11224*
Irregular | Building 75x90

This congregation in southern Brooklyn closed in July 2025, and I was tipped off to the closing by my friends Shelley and Mike Braff, who live nearby to the shul. (My friend Brian Solomon also went here as a young boy.) Mike had attended Hebrew School here and was a bar mitzvah. At some point the synagogue was known as Gemilas Chesed.From the outside, the building is a bland, post WW2 construction but inside it had many nice details. The foyer had an interesting Jewish star pattern on the walls. The lower level had several pretty pieces of artwork on the walls, in addition to many plaques with memorial tablets. It was a Conservative congregation. An early childhood school moved in when the shul vacated. A particularly poignant sight in the basement was a memorial plaque tablet from the 31st Street Talmud Torah. Long gone, and where will this go now?

# More Former Synagogues and Jewish Institutions in Queens

My book *The Lost Synagogues of the Bronx and Queens* was published in 2011. Since that time, two more Queens synagogues have closed their doors and a few others have been repurposed by other Jewish groups. I also found a few more former shuls and a school that I had not covered previously. The former synagogues in Queens that I document here date back to various decades: some are post mid-century while others are closer to a century old, if not older. Their more recent usage varies: two became churches, one is a private home, a few became schools or community centers.

*Agudas Israel*
*1618 Cornelia Street (near Wyckoff Avenue) | 11385*
Regular | Building 42x75 | 1 Story | Built 1931

This building ceased to house a congregation decades ago, but it still closely resembles a synagogue; the people who moved in and turned it into a private residence have retained much of the exterior. Jewish stars still appear in stained glass windows on the front and sides. The name of the shul is still present, in English. A metal Jewish star sculpture is atop a small pediment above the entrance. The building does seem faded and weathered but it is intriguing.

The American Synagogue Directory of 1960 placed this synagogue in Brooklyn; it was considered part of Bushwick but later designated as a part of Ridgewood, Queens. They were led by Rabbi Benjamin Sharfman and President Irving Alter. One of the more unusual aspects of this former synagogue, which is a moderate sized building, is that it backs onto a different street: due to its placement on a narrow street, the former Congregation

Agudas Israel fronts on Cornelia Street and backs onto Jefferson Avenue. From the Jefferson Avenue side, it just appears to be a private home. I was inside once, in the mid 2010s, and the people who lived there (a married couple who were artists and teachers) showed me how they were renovating parts of the main sanctuary.

*Garden Jewish Center*
*24–20 Parsons Blvd. (at 144th Street) | 11357*

Mid Century Modern presides here. The building is a one-level structure, faced in grayish stone, and it backs onto another street. Up until sometime in 2014 the name of the synagogue was spelled out over the main entrance. The first time that I visited the congregation had closed, and I saw piles of unopened mail inside the foyer. The GJC lasted over 50 years, closed in 2012 and merged with the Bay Terrace Jewish Center. The American Synagogue Directory of 1960 lists their rabbi as Martin L. Applebaum and the president as Frank Reiter. Martin Cooper was their final rabbi. It had a Sunday morning basketball league and Veterans of Foreign Wars meetings.

*Bayside Jewish Center*
*203–5 32nd Avenue (between 203rd-204th Streets) | 11361*

This midcentury campus of stone and brick covers a full avenue block; it has a parking lot as well. So different from the majority of NYC synagogues in style, this very suburban-looking site featured a lovely Judaica-themed sculpture attached to the exterior of the sanctuary section of the main building. Included in that sculpture was a Decalogue, a menorah, open Torah scroll, a crown and more. According to Google Maps, it was removed from the building sometime after 2016. If you look carefully from the sidewalk, you can still see parts of the stained glass windows of the main sanctuary. (Go inside and ask politely to see them now.) The synagogue was organized in 1926 and first located in a storefront. Another congregation joined up with them in 1935. Their earlier site was a few blocks away but they moved to the 203rd Street site and this building dates to 1960. A.H. Salkowitz was the architect of this building, and he won an award for the project. The American Synagogue Directory of 1960 lists their rabbi as Dr. William A. Orentlicher and the president was H. Howard Ostrin.

*Beth El*
*30–85 35th Street | 11103*
Regular | Building 57x88 | 2 Stories | Masonry | Built 1928

A few visible Jewish stars remain on the front of the former Beth El in Astoria. The three rather impressive examples are found in the trio of windows above the main doors. There is another Jewish star in a window guard by the sidewalk, to the right of the entrance. There are three more small Jewish stars on poles by the alleyway. I was inside this building once, in the mid 2010s, and saw other stained glass windows from the days of the synagogue. The building now houses a Baptist church. The original site of the Congregation Beth-El was on the southeast corner of Astoria Boulevard and 37th Street, 1927. This building dates to 1928. The American Synagogue Directory of 1960 lists their rabbi as Ephraim Shimoff.

*Conservative Synagogue of Jamaica Estates*
*182–69 Wexford Terrace (at Dalny Road) | 11432*
Irregular | Building 80x80 | 2 stories | Built 1968

The Decalogue on the front of this building, which is rendered in Hebrew, is among the largest Decalogues that I have seen on a synagogue, active or former. Add to that the several Jewish stars on the railings by the steps and path, and you might be confused about the affiliation of this building. But it also reads "Fresh Anointing International Church" underneath the Decalogue, which updates the situation. This corner building is done in pale tan stucco. Toward the back of the complex there is a small metal plaque that reads "The Daniel Kanfer Chapel," a dedication from the synagogue days. This congregation merged together with two others in the general area in the early 2000s.

*Yeshiva of Central Queens*
*90–40 150th Street | 11435*
Building 166x89 | 5 stories | Masonry | Built 1961

It is not surprising that a former yeshiva or day school would later be turned into a public school building. That is the story with the former Yeshiva of Central Queens, which later was turned into ALC– Jamaica Academy. These two sandy colored brick buildings have a boxy, institutional style with a few interesting clues to its past: one plaque reads "This building was erected through the generosity of Mr. & Mrs. Daniel Reisman" and the other "Yeshiva of Central Queens 1947." The yeshiva has since moved elsewhere in Queens, to Kew Gardens Hills.

*First Independent Hebrew Congregation of Jamaica*
*90–21 160th Street | 11432*
Regular | Building 40x60 | 2 stories |
Reinforced concrete | Built 1931

This building has endured a variety of changes over time and has a hodgepodge feel to it, especially in the front. But there is at least one Jewish star remaining on the exterior, on the front of the staircase. There is also a cornerstone that reads "1905." According to Google Maps, this building was still used by a Baptist church at least through July 2018, but by November 2020 that was gone, and the building was undergoing renovations. By September 2022 the Green Care Center was in this space, and had repainted a few Jewish stars. (Now red, at some point the stars were medium blue.) The alternative name of this congregation was Ahavas Israel, organized in 1900. The 1940s tax photo shows that the front of the shul had many more windows and decorative details that by the 1980s tax photo had been removed or covered over.

*Congregation Beth Israel of Richmond Hill*
*92–91 102nd Street | 11418*
Corner

I found out about the closing of this synagogue from a friend named Ron. During one of the final days it was open, I visited the building and spoke with Ron, his wife and two friends of theirs. I took some memorabilia from the congregation (anniversary journals, bulletins, a copy of the by-laws, a binder with Board meeting minutes (1978–1982), and more. There were several memorial plaque boards on the walls, many pretty stained glass windows with names. The congregation began in 1910. From the outside their building resembled a house that had been modified into a synagogue, with many stained glass windows and a seven-branched menorah design above the main entrance. By the time I arrived the lawn was quite overgrown and the front steps had damage. One red cornerstone had "5675" and "1914" chiseled into its sides. (They dedicated the building in 1914.) The congregation was leaving behind various items such as the windows.

# More Former Synagogues in the Bronx

My book The Lost Synagogues of the Bronx and Queens was published in 2011 and since that time I have located more former synagogues, especially in the Bronx. A few actually closed since 2011, and others I found out about after the book was published. These buildings are found in several Bronx neighborhoods. Property data is included from the NYC Department of Finance website.

*Temple Emanuel of Parkchester*
*2000 Benedict Avenue (at Pugsley Avenue) | 10462*
Irregular | SE corner | Building 70x92 |
2 stories | Built 1949

This building is an extended set of boxy sections, with some interesting remainders from its days as the Temple. Despite the simple entrance, there are nice touches such as a cornerstone reading "1948," the name Temple Emanuel (obscured by plants), and the beautiful cast stone sculpture featuring two Lions of Judah flocking a Decalogue. But also look carefully at the series of stained glass memorial windows, which you can read from outside (albeit in reverse). On the Benedict Avenue side there is still a synagogue announcement board. The building ceased being a synagogue on October 31, 2011, after nearly 80 years. Among the rabbis that served the congregation were Lublin, Mandelcorn, Tumim, Spevack, and Romm. They worked with more than a dozen student rabbis over the years. According to the American Synagogue Directory of 1960, the temple president then was Samuel P. Parness.

*Carmel Synagogue*
*1780 Seward Avenue (at St. Lawrence Avenue) | 10473*
Regular | SE corner | Building 27x100 |
2 stories | Built 1943

This brick corner building is a basic rectangle, scrubbed of its exterior Judaica except for two Jewish stars. One is noticeable, precisely at the building's edge, and one is harder to see, on the St. Lawrence Avenue side. There are a few spaces on the front of the building that were likely dedication plaques, but they have been painted over. According to the Bronx Synagogues website, this synagogue was organized in 1928. In the 1940s Tax photo you can see that the building was only one story in height; it isn't clear when they built upward. According to the American Synagogue Directory of 1960, they were led by Rabbi Maurice L. Schwartz and the synagogue president was Morris E. Tonelson.

*Jewish Center of Pelham Bay*
*1807 Mahan Avenue (near Buhre Avenue) | 10461*
Regular | Building 40x86 | 1 story | Built 1944

This small brick building fits in cozily with the private houses that dominate this street. The primary Jewish identifiers that remain here are the two Jewish stars on the front gate. If you scrutinize the front of the building, you can see a few faded bits of Hebrew letters and Jewish stars. The brick work has some nice patterns. According to the American Synagogue Directory of 1960 the rabbi then was Joseph J. Lichtenstein and the shul president was Eugene Schessler.

*Throggs Neck Jewish Center*
*2916 Lafayette Avenue | 10465*
Building 35x70 | 1 story | Built 1922

On a quiet block of private homes, this small former shul is actually one of the more subdued buildings. A faded sign near the roofline states the name of the shul, with a Jewish star. Each side of the building also has one small Jewish star near the roofline. According to the Bronx Synagogues website, this synagogue was organized in 1924. Bertha and Mark Corets were founding members of the Throggs Neck Jewish Center, a synagogue located within walking distance of their home. They helped greatly in keeping the congregation afloat in the early years of the Great Depression. The synagogue survived at least into the late 1990s. It had been the only synagogue in the neighborhood.

*Hunts Point Chevra Bikur Cholim*
*823 Faile Street (near Gilbert Place) | 10474*
Regular | Building 27x75 | 3 stories | Built 1930

You need to look carefully to see the one remaining Jewish star on the front of this former synagogue. It's a boxy building that has been largely stripped of its Judaic past.

According to Bronx Synagogues this synagogue was organized in 1929 and dedicated in 1934.

In the 1940s tax photo you can see the original Jewish star rose window near the roofline. Apparently at some point there was a Reform synagogue across the street from this building.

According to the American Synagogue Directory of 1960 they were led by Rabbi Samuel Orenstein and the synagogue president was Max Fink.

*Mercaz HaRav*
*2832 Valentine Avenue (near East 197th Street) | 10458*
Regular | Building 21 x 55 | 2 stories | Built 1931

This building is a bit of a hodge-podge, with a front extension that does not seem to be part of the original building. However, that is where you can still see significant remaining Judaica.

(My guess is the items were moved to this part of the building later on.) At the peak of the front there is a metal Jewish star sculpture; a few feet below it are two tablets or filled in windows, each with a small Jewish star; a scratched out sign still reads "Cong. Mercaz Harav" and below that, a painted-over brick Jewish star. There is even a memorial tablet with Hebrew, but some of the letters are hard to read. According to Bronx Synagogues this congregation was organized in 1929. In the 1940s tax photo, the main front doors were more stylish; at some point these were altered. A martial arts school is now located here.

*Community Center of Israel*
*2440 Esplanade (near Pearsall Avenue) | 10469*
Irregular | corner | Buildings 56 x 82 |
1 story | Masonry | Built 1952

What will become of the lengthy campus of buildings that constituted the former Community Center of Israel? Situated on an unusually shaped plot of land, this post WW2 brick complex has been abandoned, and the beautiful stained glass windows on the Pearsall Avenue side are deteriorating. The front still has significant Judaica such as the congregational name in English, Jewish stars in a few different patterns, a Decalogue, an eight-branch menorah sculpture attached to the building, a plaque with the *Ma Tovu* quote (from Numbers 24:5), a Jewish star on a railing, and even a cornerstone with the year 1950 and the Hebrew year. But there is also graffiti, boarded up windows, and other reminders of its deterioration. According to Bronx Synagogues, the congregation was organized in 1954. And in the American Synagogue Directory of 1960 we learn that the rabbi was Simon I. Konovitch and the temple president was Leo S.Marcus.

*Young Israel of Mosholu Parkway*
*100 East 208th Street (at Steuben Avenue) | 10467*
*(aka 3231 Steuben Avenue)*
Irregular | Building 25x90 | 2 stories | Built 1956 | Masonry

One of the more peculiar-looking lost synagogues in the Bronx is this campus, which is essentially a boxy main building with a connector and front extension. The main building, of sandy brick, still has the Hebrew "Beit Yitzhak V'Rikvah" and in English, "The Becky and Isidor Jacobson Building." To the left of this is an interesting abstract pattern made of concrete. The middle of the extension has a set of unusual six-sided windows, with stained glass designs. The white main entrance has a sign for the church but underneath that it reads "Young Israel of Mosholu Parkway" with the Young Israel symbol in a triangle. (In fact, I remember it that way when I first visited this area.) There is also a small cornerstone "Dec 1952". According to Google Maps, the Young Israel name was still visible through 2018. According to the Bronx Synagogues website, this shul was built on the site of a private home that was knocked down. In 2013 the synagogue faced a heavy blow when three of its Torah scrolls were stolen. At the time the rabbi of the YI was Zevulun Charlop. At the time of this crime, it was the last remaining synagogue in the vicinity, Community Board 7.

*Ahavath(s) Achim*
*1524 Parker Street | 10462*
Building 57x75 | 1 story | Built 1925

This is a slightly unusual design for a modestly sized synagogue: two entrances at each end of the building. Above both doorways is a Decalogue and a Jewish star, although one of the Decalogues has held up better than the other (the Hebrew is legible on one, not the other). Looking at the building from the front it seems small but look at it from the alleyway and it goes back further. The sandy colored brick has held up nicely, as have other decorative details of the exterior. According to Bronx Synagogues, this synagogue was organized in 1919 and dedicated in 1925. In the 1940s tax photo, there was a sign on the front of the building, above the trio of windows. In the American Synagogue Directory of 1960 they were helmed by Rabbi Solomon Pines and the synagogue president was Max Levine.

*Morris Park Hebrew Center*
*1812 Paulding Avenue | 10461*
Irregular | Building 43x78 | 1 story | Masonry | Built 1952

This is a plain, squat red-brick building that lacks charm, except for one remainder of its days as a synagogue. There is a cornerstone with Hebrew and secular dates and a Jewish star. If you peek behind the small awning over the entrance, you can see the synagogue's name. At least until 2007 there was a Jewish star above the main doors. According to Bronx Synagogues the synagogue was organized in 1928. The American Synagogue Directory of 1960 informs us that the rabbi then was Wallace Pruzansky and the president was Nat Rosenstein.

*Van Nest Hebrew Congregation B'nai Jacob*
*1712 Garfield Street (near Van Nest Avenue) | 10460*
Regular | Building 27x75 | 2 stories | Built 1930

There is something very classic New York about this former synagogue: it embodies a type of "tenement style" former synagogue. Around New York

City (and elsewhere) you can find former and active synagogues that are similar to this one: basically a two-story brick house, with various Jewish adornments. From top to bottom, there are Jewish stars at the roofline, in stained glass windows, partially hidden at the main doors, and in a prominent rose window. There is also a small cornerstone that reads "1905," to the left of the main entrance. The building has a well-kept exterior and is charming. In the American Synagogue Directory of 1960 we learn that the rabbi then was Lazar Meskin and the president was Tanc Comras. The building was sold to a church in 1979.

*Educational Jewish Center*
*805 Astor Avenue (at Barnes Avenue) | 10467*
Irregular | NE corner | Building 76x80 |
1 story Masonry | Built 1930

This red-brick, corner building does not look all that remarkable, until you catch a glimpse of the stained glass windows along the wall painted white: those are from the days of the synagogue, and are similar to those found in a few other former synagogues in Brooklyn, According to Google Maps, sometime before 2014 you could see a concrete Jewish star above the main doors. Above the church sign there is a simple Decalogue design. It seems to have been painted over several times so it isn't as noticeable as in previous years. The American Synagogue Directory of 1960 lists the rabbi as Louis A. Strinhorn.

*Netzach Israel B'nai Jacob*
*1078 Kelly Street (near East 167th Street) | 10459*
Masonry | Year built 1930 | Building 44x100 1 story

This pretty former synagogue, with its triple door entrance and scalloped decorative touches, resembles former synagogues in parts of Brooklyn, such as the former Rishon L'Tzion on East 95th Street. That style was apparently popular in the 1920s. There are a couple of Jewish stars noticeable, as well as two menorahs and most importantly, the synagogue name in Hebrew over the center door. This congregation was organized in 1914 and the alternate name was Preserve Israel. It was also spelled "Netsach" in the JGSNY website listing. In the 1940s tax photo you can see additional building details, such as an English sign featuring the congregation's name, a smaller additional sign above one of the front entrance doors, and the Jewish star rose window was quite elaborate in design. According to the American Synagogue Directory of 1960, they were led by Rabbi Lipa Eidelman and the shul president was Herman Mostel.

# Former Long Island Synagogues: Nassau and Suffolk Counties

The eastern suburbs of New York City, Nassau and Suffolk Counties, have a number of former synagogues located in various towns. Some of the buildings have stylistic similarities to former (and active) synagogues in Queens, the NYC borough to which they are closest in proximity. Others are quite different, and have more in common with suburban synagogues in other states.

These two suburbs are the ones with which I am most familiar, and I was familiar with at least two of these buildings when they were active congregations. I had driven past the one in Elmont many times, because it is near the Beth David Cemetery where members of my family are buried, and I attended a bat mitzvah and a bar mitzvah at one other lost synagogue in the area.

Some of the buildings I visited have since been knocked down. A few I saw have been altered so greatly that I chose not to include them here.

I am especially grateful to Brad Kolodny, author of Seeking Sanctuary: 125 Years of Synagogues on Long Island, for his own research and also assisting me with my investigation of the lost synagogues of LI. He also maintains a fascinating Facebook page dedicated to "Long Island Jewish History".

## NASSAU COUNTY

*Congregation Tifereth Israel*
*7 Continental Place | Glen Cove | 11542*

This may not be the largest former synagogue on Long Island, but it appears expansive because it is set back on a raised plot of land, with two sets of staircases that lead up to this elegant brick building. The main entrance, with three arches and two classical columns, is well kept and there are nice brick details all around. Over that entrance it still says "Congregation Tifereth Israel" in English. There are two date signs, one "1917" (the year it was built) and the other "1959." The sides of the building have several nice stained glass windows from the time of the synagogue. I was able to visit inside (during a soup kitchen session) and saw that the main sanctuary has light fixtures and lamps from the days of the synagogue. "CTI" is the oldest continuously operating Jewish congregation on Long Island and now has a different location in town. Rabbi Emmanuel Rackman was their first full-time clergyman.

*Temple B'nai Israel*
*471 Elmont Road | Elmont | 11003*

I have driven past this site several times, when it was still a synagogue and then when it became a church, due to its proximity to the Beth David Cemetery. The church there now has retained a good deal of the original exterior Judaica. The most prominent piece is the circular window with a menorah design inside it. The name Temple B'nai Israel, in English, can still be seen over the main entrance. There is a cornerstone with Hebrew and English, featuring the Hebrew word *L'chvod H*" (To the Glory of God). Also see a brass plaque above the doorway that reads "Florence and Barry Friedberg In Gratitude for Past and Present Generosity". This red brick building is not that remarkable otherwise but it is nicely maintained. The synagogue was dedicated in 1951. The American Synagogue Directory lists their rabbi as Abraham Ruderman and their president as Herbert J. Cohn.The Reform synagogue resided here for about 70 years and the final rabbi was Samuel Kehati, who served for more than 40 years. They shuttered their doors in 2022.

*Union Reform Temple*
*475 N Brookside Avenue | Freeport | 11520*

This brown brick building is intimidating, with few windows. It's brutalist architecture, for sure. But there is one Jewish remainder; the cornerstone reads *L'cvod Adonai* and "Union Reform Temple 5720 1960." The architect was Percival Goodman; he was considered to be one of the most prolific synagogue architects in the United States. In 2000 the temple merged with

Oceanside's Temple Avodah. Prior to this building they worshiped in a former church.

*Congregation Beth David*
*188 Vincent Avenue (near Merrick Road) | Lynbrook | 11563*

This two-building campus, a synagogue along with an additional building, still looks impressive from outside. But in November 2022 I stopped by and was able to walk inside, quite easily, to see serious dishevelment inside the main sanctuary and front foyer. From the outside, this main building is of brown brick, with two dome-topped towers. One of the domes has a Jewish star, and there is a Jewish star and two Decalogues above the entrance. A cornerstone gives the precise dedication date of "Aug. 12, 1928." According to the American Synagogue Directory of 1960 they were led by Rabbi Morris S. Friedman and President Arthur Kain.

When I ventured inside it was chilling: disarray, cracked stained glass memorial windows (as well as others in good shape), peeling plaster, and lots of debris. There was also a nice looking but worn Holy Ark, a *Modim* prayer poster, and a kitschy menorah that looked like a set of trombones. The smaller building still has the name "Beth David" above the entrance, with two Jewish stars beside it. There is a small brass plaque dedicated to a curbside tree, dated from 1994. The congregation is now located elsewhere as B'nai Sholom-Beth David.

*New Hyde Park JCC*
*100 Lakeville Road | New Hyde Park | 11040*

The elongated building that was New Hyde Park Jewish Community Center is not a remarkable structure, but it has several interesting pieces left over from its Jewish past. There are several stained glass memorial windows remaining, with names. There is a prominent Jewish star window visible above the secondary entrance. There is a Decalogue above the main entrance. I spotted at least one door jamb where a *mezuzah* had been removed. Inside the main sanctuary has pretty windows, and the Hindu congregation there now has maintained it well, while adding their own items. The synagogue opened its doors here in 1932. The American Synagogue Directory of 1960 lists Rabbi David Moseson as their spiritual head. According to a Jewish

Telegraphic Agency article in 2004, this congregation merged with the larger Shelter Rock Jewish Center in Roslyn.

*Roosevelt Jewish Center*
*55 Mansfield Place | Roosevelt | 11575*

This streamlined building is now the Roosevelt Youth Center and has an interesting mural on the front. It also has its shul cornerstone: it reads "1963 5723". Their history does precede this date: according to Long Island Jewish historian Brad Kolodny, they incorporated in 1932 and built their synagogue in 1937. They are listed at this address in the American Synagogue Directory of 1960, with Rabbi Harry Z. Schectman and President Charles D. Wertheim. Radio and media personality Howard Stern was a bar mitzvah here, and in 1967 the congregation merged with B'nai Israel in Freeport.

*Community Reform Temple*
*712 The Plain Road | Westbury | 11590*

The former Community Reform Temple does not look like a typical house of worship. Basically it is a boxy building with big windows and several parking spaces. Although it is now used by an Asian spirituality group, there are remaining Jewish clues on view. As of late 2022 there was a *mezuzah* by the front door and a cornerstone that reads "5735 1975" with the Hebrew letters as well. There appeared to be some remaining Judaica inside but I couldn't categorize it. This building opened in 1975. According to Google Maps, this was still a synagogue in July 2019.

*Shaarei Shalom East Bay Reform Temple*
*2569 Merrick Rd | Bellmore | 11710*

Admittedly this is a peculiarly shaped building, a post-WW2 construction. It still has some Judaica remaining, such as a rusty *mezuzah* by the main doors, and a stained glass window panel above the main doors that reads *Shaarei Shalom* in Hebrew, with a simple design. Using Google Maps, one can see that even in 2012 the name of the synagogue was still emblazoned on the Merrick Road side of the building, along with a menorah.

## SUFFOLK COUNTY

*Amityville Hebrew Association*
*39 Greene Avenue | Amityville | 11701*

This is a plain box of a building, with five pretty lancet windows and a matching doorway. I'm not sure what actually remains from the synagogue's days. This building was earlier known as Fraternity Hall. The congregation was later called Beth Sholom Center and built another home. According to the American Synagogue Directory of 1960, they were helmed by Rabbi Leon Spielman.

# Former Central and Upstate New York Synagogues

New York State has long been home to Jewish communities beyond New York City. Several of these communities were (and are) in medium and small sized urban areas, while others have been suburban or rural. In many places the buildings and their campuses have been expansive compared to those seen in the congested sections of Manhattan, Brooklyn and the Bronx, but there are exceptions. The farming communities, the industrial areas, and suburban commuters built synagogues in a variety of sizes and styles.

Buffalo, Rochester, Oswego, Orange, Syracuse, Albany, Schenectady, Newburgh, the Catskills, Rockland, Westchester and other parts of New York are home to former synagogues that reflect a variety of styles. There are huge edifices, and modestly scaled sites too, and while they often share similarities with New York City shul buildings, there are noticeable differences as well. They were and are important to their greater communities, and especially to the Jewish groups that settled there.

The fortunes of these congregations have waxed, waned, and changed in many ways. Just as in New York City, and elsewhere in the United States, congregations have opened and closed, moved elsewhere and merged together, expanded and taken less typical routes. A major influence on the Jewish communities in some sections of this region was the Erie Canal.The ups and downs of a variety of industries also impacted the fortunes of their communities and in turn, their synagogues. You could compare the fate of an industrial Pennsylvania town and its synagogue such as Shamokin to that of Newburgh in Orange County, New York, for example.

My first serious foray into documenting upstate New York former shuls was during the summer of 2020, when I visited Syracuse. The primary reason was to cover musical instrument stores, for a music industry website. I wrote a few stories each year for The Music & Sound Retailer, for a period of five years. (These pieces were published under a pseudonym.) In Syracuse, I surveyed four music stores, and also visited a few former synagogues. In fact, I stayed overnight in a rather pleasant hotel that was built as a synagogue. I found two other former synagogues in the city, one that became a messianic church and another that became a different type of church.

The following year, I did research on a building on Abeel Street in Kingston, which I had wondered about when driving past it two or three times, and found out that it too had been built as a synagogue. This building, now a residence, is a short trip away from New Paltz, where my older daughter attended college at SUNY New Paltz.

During the spring and summer of 2023 I took three significant excursions in and north of Westchester County, and to central and northern New York, with the main purpose of documenting former synagogues. My "Capital District Plus " day trip on May 30 consisted of Schenectady, Albany, East Schodack, Hudson, Poughkeepsie, Newburgh and Haverstraw.

The second trip further north was the first part of the multi-day trip I took from upstate New York, into Pennsylvania, Ohio, and then Michigan. On Independence Day, I drove to Nyack, then Rome, Oswego, and Rochester. The next day I visited Buffalo and Tonawanda. For the third trip, July 25, I covered Yorktown Heights, Peekskill, Warwick, as well as a few areas further south in White Plains and Yonkers. The former synagogues I documented on these days vary in size, design, and current condition.

After breaking my leg in April 2024 I took time off from making field trips, but resumed in August 2024 with trips to Mount Vernon (and nearby Bronx), and then in early January 2025 I travelled to Newburgh, Ossining and Mount Vernon again, to document a few more locations after finding additional online resources with addresses. And in May 2025 I found out that yet another Yonkers congregation had closed,so I visited it with a friend.

Many of these former synagogues are now used as churches. A few have become residences, commercial establishments, schools, non-profit and community centers. A few sat empty when I saw them. Most of these buildings still retain exterior Judaica, such as decalogues, Hebrew writing, Jewish stars, stained glass windows, and the like. One was rotting away so badly that when I entered it (rather gingerly, I might add) I choked back tears. Many did remind me of an assortment of synagogue buildings I have seen in New York City; they share stylistic elements and certainly names. I have encountered many former synagogues named Beth Israel, and B'nai/ Sons/Brothers of Israel, for example.

Occasionally I encounter former synagogues that are located on streets that had name changes, which makes it a bit tricky to find them. (This has also happened in New York City and other cities.) A few of the former synagogues had been built originally as churches; a situation seen in New York City as well.

## BUFFALO

*Ahavas Achim-Lubavitz*
*345 Tacoma Avenue (near Colvin Avenue) | 14216*

The two buildings that make up the former Ahavas Achim-Lubavitz are bland but well-kept brick buildings, and they do have some interesting Judaic reminders. The smaller building (#351) has a cornerstone reading "1961–5721" with a Jewish star; the main building has a few Jewish stars on the side, and you can see one or two of those on Colvin Avenue, if you gaze through someone's driveway. This is located in a quiet residential area. As you might realize by the hyphenated name, the congregation resulted from the merger of two separate congregations: Ahavas Achim and Anshe Lubavitz. This building was designed by Jack Kushin and built in 1951. According to the American Synagogue Directory of 1960 they were led by Rabbi Alvin M. Marcus and President Samuel Benatovich. A later rabbi was Leonard M.Buchen. Journalist and TV personality Wolf Blitzer attended this congregation when young.

*Temple Beth El*
*151(5) Richmond Avenue (near York Street) | 14222*

The former Beth El stands on a bucolic street of private houses. This brown brick building is in nice condition,with visible Judaica remaining (two Jewish stars on the front entrance and lots of stained glass windows with certain Jewish details). If you walk further back from the building you will see the dome atop the center. It also has a semi-circular driveway in front, not a typical detail. There is a vague similarity between this former synagogue and that of a former synagogue in Toledo, Ohio, as far as the windows and layout. This is the oldest congregation in the city, dating back to 1847, and was first known as Congregation Bethel. They actually received funds from the illustrious, long-established Touro family of Rhode Island. This building dates to 1911 and was designed by Henry Osgood Holland. But later the congregation moved to Tonawanda (and that building will be discussed here too). The final service held here was in October 1966. The American Synagogue Directory of 1960 lists their rabbi as Milton Feierstein and their president as Harry Seeberg. Beth El merged into what is now Temple Beth Tzedek in nearby Williamsville.

*Temple Emanu-El*
*385 Colvin Avenue | 14216*

All that remains of this building now is an old-fashioned tower, set behind a garden apartment complex. Emanu-El was founded in 1924, and this building was originally a church. It was renovated into a synagogue by architect Louis Greenstein. It was considered Modern Orthodox and later became Conservative. In 1968 Emanu-El merged with another local congregation, Temple Beth David-Ner Israel, and they became Shaarey Zedek, now located in the suburbs. According to the American Synagogue Directory of 1960 they were led by Rabbi Isaac Klein and President Joseph H. Reingold.

*Brith Israel-Anshe Emes*
*1237 Hertel Avenue | 14216*

Up until at least 2020, according to Google Maps, this was a light-colored brick building, of a simple design, with Judaica on the front such as a Jewish star with a Decalogue and menorah designs beneath it. It had been used by a church group for many years. Now this building has been painted black and businesses reside inside. There are at least two remainders from the Jewish days: a cornerstone that reads "ERECTED 1955–5716" with a small Jewish star, and a memorial plaque, partially covered by a decorative water fountain, for a Morris Simon. The plaque is in English and Hebrew, and Mr.Simon was actually part of the Anshe (A)mes group that merged into this congregation. Two Orthodox congregations merged together and became this one shul. Jack Kushin designed this site, which was built from 1953–1955. The American Synagogue Directory of 1960 lists the rabbi as the Reverend Simon Solomon.

*Temple Beth El*
*2368 Eggert Road | 14150 Tonawanda*

When Beth El moved to the suburbs, it built this site. On one side, the former Beth El is set back from a residential strip of single family homes; and on the other there are several commercial establishments. Beth El seems almost like a former commercial establishment rather than a former synagogue, but there's a cross atop a Jewish star to the left of the main entrance. There is also a cornerstone reading "Temple Beth El" in English and in Hebrew, as well as "1960–5720." The site endured a major fire in 1978 and it was rebuilt. In 2008 the congregation merged with Temple Shaarey Zedek and became Temple Beth Zedek. The lengthy brick building seems to be in good shape and is used by a church.

## ROCHESTER

*Leopold Street Schule*
*30 Leopold Street (at Harrison Street) | 14605*

One of the more uniquely styled former synagogues in New York State is this gem, which still has its official name, Congregation Beth Israel, visible in a plaque set behind the main doors. A cornerstone reads "1886" and this makes it also one of the older shul buildings within New York State. The elaborate, eclectic front is really what makes this an atypical and special building, such as the sloping shapes in the front section and the elaborate ironwork. Although it is not far from the housing development Chatham Gardens, this building is surrounded by big parking lots and industrial facilities, so it seems a bit forlorn, even if it is used now as a church. It's no surprise that this site is a designated National Landmark. In the American Synagogue Directory of 1960 the leaders listed were Rabbi Samuel A. Baker and President Joe H. Lazarus.

*Talmud Torah/Beth Haknesses*
*122 Chatham Gardens (near Joseph Avenue) | 14605*

It's not easy to find this former synagogue building, until you realize that it is enveloped by a housing complex. It is across from the residents' parking lots. The front has been greatly modified but does have stylistic elements of certain early 1900s synagogues. There is a simple cornerstone near the front doors that reads "1913."

*Congregation B'nai Israel*
*692 Joseph Avenue (near Loomis Street) | 14621*

Sadly, this stately former synagogue became so dilapidated that most of it was demolished– even though it had been placed on the National Register in 2015. The front section has been retained. When I visited in July 2023, I saw a once regal brick building that looked disheveled from the front, but was in terrible shape in the back and inside. I entered the building through a broken door and saw pretty stained glass windows and memorial plaques, amidst distressing conditions such as huge sinkholes. Pews were knocked down, staircases rotted out, broken glass and plaster segments strewn about. It was a horror. Apparently there had been at least one fire there, leading to the deterioration. Also known as Congregation Ahavas Achim Anshi Austria, this Orthodox congregation was established in 1928. The site was used as a shul until 2004. There had been plans to turn it into a community center with various activities, but the condition was too dire. The American Synagogue Directory of 1960 lists Rabbi Henry Hyman and President Nathan Goldstein as their leaders.

## OSWEGO

*Congregation Adath Israel*
*39 East Oneida Street/163 East 3rd Street | 13126*

On a sizable parcel of land, Washington Square, can be found the former Adath Israel. This quaint brick building has a community playground behind it. It is not your typical old synagogue building, neither a modest rowhouse nor a neoclassical (or Byzantine) styled structure. It looks more like a modified home. It still reads "Congregation Adath Israel" over the main door, and there is a prominent Jewish star above the biggest window on the front. There are other nice stained glass windows on the sides. This site was built in 1831 and served first as a Baptist church. It is one of the oldest buildings in Oswego. The American Synagogue Directory of 1960 lists Rabbi Norman H. Nass and President Leon Shapiro as their leaders.

## ROME

*Adas Israel*
*705 Hickory Street (near Roser Terrace) | 13440*

The former Adas Israel building sits amidst a lot of space: it has a large parking lot to the side and a sports field in the back.This midcentury building of brick is mostly remarkable for its entrance: large, clear windows with a big Jewish star. To the side there is a cornerstone, a bit difficult to locate, that reads "1960/ 5720". Rabbi Manfred Wimer and President Benjamin Shulkin are listed in the American Synagogue Directory of 1960. The rabbi served this congregation for 34 years, but died at age 89 in Maryland.

## NYACK

*Congregation Sons of Israel*
*67 South Broadway (at Hudson Avenue) 10960*

Set on a corner of the town's main road, the former Sons of Israel is a modest-sized brick and stone building with Jewish stars on its various parts. It resembles several NYC former shuls.There are a few Jewish stars on the front (on a turret and in a stained glass window), at the back (on the turrets again), and pretty stained glass windows all over. A small white cornerstone reads "1924" and "5684" in a pretty font. This building was dedicated in September 1925. They outgrew this site and built the current building which opened in 1967, on North Broadway. According to the American Synagogue Directory of 1960 their leaders were Rabbi Irwin H. Fishbein and President Louis Sakoff. The congregation still exists: www.csinyack.org

## SYRACUSE

*Temple Adath Yeshurun*
*601 South Crouse Avenue (at Harrison Street) | 13210*

This is a wonderful version of the neoclassical American synagogue. Built of sandy brick on a slightly raised corner, with four big pillars and a pediment with a Jewish star in the middle, this still presents itself as a synagogue but it had a stint as a performing arts center and is now a hotel. The Hebrew quote from Psalms, *Pitkhu li shaare zedek avo vam odeh yah* is paired with

"Open Ye portals of Righteousness I will enter and praise God." This former synagogue is just a few blocks away from Beth Israel, also on Harrison Street. The congregation moved into this building in 1922 but its history goes back further. The architect was Gordon Wright. "TAY" as they are called moved out in 1968. The American Synagogue Directory of 1960 lists their leaders as Rabbi Irwin I. Hyman and President Asher S. Markson. The congregation is now located elsewhere within the city. In the summer of 2020 I stayed here one night, in a large room with windows that evoked the upper section of the synagogue, because that was its former usage.

*Beth El*
*3528 East Genesee Street (at Carlton Drive) | 13214*

Overall this sprawling former synagogue is not remarkable in design, but it has a few pieces of Judaica that make it worth investigating. On the wall to the left of the main entrance, there is a curious and bittersweet collection of cornerstones, from former sites and the congregations that merged into this building, such as "Temple Beth-El 5725–1965" and "Congregation Beth Israel 1854–1925" and "Congregation Poale Zedek Erected 1896". Interestingly the Poale Zedek stone has the congregational name in Hebrew but the other words are in English. Another wonderful feature on the exterior is the Twelve Tribes wall decoration, just around the corner from those cornerstones, a series of panels in a midcentury style.

*Temple Beth Israel*
*601 Irving Avenue (at Harrison Street) | 13210*

Located on a corner which goes uphill on the Harrison Street side, this is a slightly jarring former synagogue that was most recently used by a messianic group. There is a curious mix of Hebrew and English above the main entrance, that was greatly rubbed out, so that only a few words in both languages are legible ("Bet" in Hebrew; "This House" in English). Above the quotes there is a Jewish star. It is a nice brick and stone building that needs upkeep, and the steps are in poor shape. Also at the front entrance there is a trio of pilasters with circles, and at least one of them has the faint design of a menorah. Peek inside the front foyer to see a tiled design on the floor that reads "Beth Israel." On the Harrison side there are still several pretty stained glass windows. The American Synagogue Directory of 1960 lists

Rabbi Jacob H. Epstein and President Abram Gordon as their leaders. According to Professor Samuel Gruber, this building was actually abandoned by the congregation in the 1960s and served for a while as a Baptist church.

## KINGSTON

*Temple Israel (Emanuel)*
*50 Abeel Street (near Wurts Street) | 12401*

The first time I drove past this building, I sensed that it had been a lost synagogue, but I had to do research to confirm this hunch. It features a split Decalogue on the upper level, with Roman numerals. There are other decorative features that give it that "onetime synagogue" feel. It also housed restaurants and bars at various times, and even a church. The building dates to 1892, and had an impressive pipe organ (which is no longer there). It moved to Albany Avenue and is now called Congregation Emanuel of the Hudson Valley.

## SCHENECTADY

*Shaarai Shamayim*
*18 North College Street (by Cottage Row) | 12305*

*Temple Gates of Heaven*
*1098 Parkwood Blvd (at Rugby Road) | 12308*

This congregation is still active but in a newer home. However, it has two local former homes that can be visited. On the North College Street location, there is one secular detail left on the building, a cornerstone that reads "1891." This brick building has a dome on the top but no obvious Judaica remaining. The Parkwood Boulevard location has more Judaica. This stately corner building looks like a comfortable house (it was actually a Christian Science temple), and it appears to have one definite ghostly reminder of its Jewish past, a faded Decalogue in the pediment above the main entrance. There are also what appear to be very faded Hebrew letters above the four columns at the main entrance; I made out a Shin and could discern a few other letters. It is the oldest Jewish congregation in Schenectady, and began in 1854. They have been in their current home since 1956, on Eastern Parkway.

*Beth Israel*
*826 State Street | 12307*

Located on a street mixed with residences and commercial units, the former Beth Israel is a modest brick building with nice touches and a streamlined, arched entrance way. It resembles many other medium-sized former and active synagogue buildings in New York and elsewhere.

A cornerstone on one side reads "5697" and the corresponding Hebrew letters (*Tet Resh Tzadi Zion)* and one on the other side reads "1937." The American Synagogue Directory of 1960 lists their leaders as Rabbi Joshua J. Epstein and President George Finke. I was able to visit inside because a family that goes there for dance class let me inside. The main sanctuary has a charming light fixture that features Jewish stars, and I have seen similar styled lights in shul buildings in New York City.

## ALBANY

*Temple Beth Emeth*
*121 Jay Street (at South Swan Street) | 12210*

A fortress of stone, wrapping around a whole block, the former Temple Beth Emeth looks like it was built for the ages. It is located across the street from a somewhat brutalist mid-century set of buildings that are a jarring contrast. But there is still a considerable amount of remaining Judaica here. There is well-preserved Hebrew writing, as well as small, faded Jewish stars. You can see pretty Jewish-star pattern windows. The cornerstone reads "1887" on one side and "5648" on the other. The familiar phrase "Mine Shall Be/ A House of Prayer/ Unto All People" is divided up above the three doorways, with the original Hebrew beneath. (*Ki Bayti Bet Tefillah Y'Karai L'Khol HaAmim*). Overall this is one of the oldest standing New York former synagogues outside of New York City, and it is very impressive. The architect was Adolph Fleischman with Isaac Perry.

*Beth El Jacob (Pastures)*
*94 Herkimer Street (near South Pearl Street) | 12202*

Except for a red church sign, this former synagogue looks so much like a Jewish institution due to all the remaining exterior Judaica. The design is a bit fanciful, especially in the segment above the main entrance. The trio of doorways is topped in the middle by "Beth El Jacob" in an arc, and above that in Hebrew, "K'K Beth El Jacob." Perhaps the most remarkable piece here is the rose window with its multiple, overlaid Jewish stars and a menorah in the middle. There are also two sets of windows that are Decalogue shaped, as well as more modestly styled windows. The building could use some upgrading (the two tower sections need a paint job). To the far left of the main entrance there is a subtle cornerstone; the street side reads "1907" and the alley side is "5667". The back of the building has another nice circular window with a double Jewish star, and other stained glass windows also have smaller Jewish stars. According to the American Synagogue Directory of 1960, they were led by Reverend Kenneth Rabineau and their president was Samuel Sutin.

## EAST SCHODACK

*East Schodack Synagogue*
*2368 East Schodack Road | 12063*

It was not easy for me to find this cozy little former synagogue, but once I did, I noticed that interesting window. That is one unusual Jewish star. . .or is it? I ended up having an interesting conversation about this building with the current owners, The Halcyon Center, who do have the original Jewish star window and some of the other remaining Judaica.

## HUDSON

*Anshe Emet*
*14 Warren Street | 12534*

If you stand on the sidewalk or the steps leading up to this building, you're liable to think it is still in use as a synagogue, although it is now home to a Baptist church. There are three prominent Jewish stars on the front of this brick former synagogue: two cast stone medallions, one on each side, and in the middle a lovely stained glass window of Jewish star with a seven branched menorah in the middle. Above that window, in Hebrew, it reads "Beth Hamedrash Anshe Emet". On the left side is a cornerstone of "5669" and on the right one that reads "1909." There are other pleasant aspects of this building, but do note that the rear of the building can be seen from Prison Alley (and you can see more of the stained glass windows from here). According to the American Synagogue Directory of 1960, they were led by Rabbi Isaac Werlin.

## POUGHKEEPSIE

*Schomre Israel/Congregation Schomre Hadat*
*16 South Bridge Street | 12601*

This brick building is not too remarkable except in the front, but look at it from further down the street and you will see the two domes on top, one on each side of the building. There are pretty stained glass memorial windows on the sides and the back of the building. There is at least one Jewish star embedded in the brick, just to the side of the main entrance, as well as two Decalogues of brick design. The American Synagogue Directory of 1960 states that they were led by Rabbi Morris Hecht and President Samuel Stein. Now the congregation is located elsewhere within Poughkeepsie.

## NEWBURGH

*Temple Beth Jacob*
*119 South Street (near Liberty Street) | 12550*

Beth Jacob was the first Jewish congregation in this city. This is a charming, small former synagogue with the name "Beth Jacob" set in a pretty font about the main entrance, in an arc. There is a small Decalogue near the roofline that has been painted over but is still visible. There are six pretty stained glass windows, three on each side of the main entrance, and that has a small domed covering. A cornerstone to the left of the entrance reads "1890". The American Synagogue Directory of 1960 lists the address as 334 Gidney Avenue; *that* building is also a lost synagogue, albeit a mid-century structure. Now they are located in another site in Newburgh.

*Congregation Agudas Achim*
*251(9) Grand Street | 12550*

Founded in 1884, this congregation resided in two former churches. This curious building was actually their second home; there is a Jewish star in a window in the back. The building is quite old but Agudas Achim moved in 1946. The American Synagogue Directory of 1960 lists the rabbi as Bernard Schwartz and the president as David. L. Friedman. Now another church resides here.

*Congregation Sons of Israel*
*25 William Street | 12550*

Look carefully at the engraved stone sign just beneath the roofline; in Hebrew it still reads clearly "Beit Haknesset B'nai Israel" and "Newburgh" in transliterated Hebrew. The building is now home to a church, but is still a formidable house of worship. Two domes top the roof and the style of this brick building could be described as modified open Torah, with the outer sections standing out slightly. The building is midblock and the surrounding buildings are old. This section of Newburgh has seen better days, and the former shul is pre-World War One.

In 1964 the nearby Agudas Achim congregation merged into Sons of Israel, but in 1970 they built a new building on North Street. In the American Synagogue Directory of 1960 their leader was listed as Rabbi Mordecai J. Simckes.

## PEEKSKILL

*First Hebrew Congregation*
*813 Main Street | 10566*

This presents now as a quaint, white-paneled small house of worship. But using Google Maps, you can see that up until at least late 2017, there was a simple brown sign over the door that read "First Hebrew Congregation" and below that in Hebrew *Kehilat Ivrit Rishonah,* the precise translation. A Jewish star crowned the top peak of the building, which is now gone. There are a few sets of lancet windows that are evocative of Decalogues, but that could be a coincidence. It is located on a block that has a small-town feel, although an apartment building complex is the next block down. The original minyan of the congregation began in 1896, and this building is from 1904. They moved elsewhere within the city.

## HAVERSTRAW

*Congregation Sons of Jacob*
*37 Clove Avenue | 10927*

When I visited this building it was abandoned. Located on a quiet residential street, the name was still present on the main doors, painted in gold leaf paint, along with two Jewish stars. The main entrance arches resemble a Decalogue. There is a small cornerstone that reads "1967." However, it is listed in the American Synagogue Directory of 1960 with this same address; Rabbi Moshe Kranzler and President Seymour Dickman led this synagogue. This congregation had roots going back to the late 1800s and had a previous home, and was one of the oldest synagogues in Rockland County. But now the empty message board is a symbol of the uncertainty of this building.

## MOUNT VERNON

*Congregation Emanu-El*
*261 East Lincoln Avenue (at Claremont Avenue) | 10552*

This is a sprawling Brutalist style brick campus that goes back a full avenue. There are some reminders of the days as a synagogue, such as pretty stained glass windows at the entrance and in the sanctuary that were from the synagogue time. But most important are the cornerstone and the quote from Deuteronomy 6, the *Shema* (a dailyprayer and affirmation). Rendered here in English, engraved just below the roofline, is the quote "Hear O Israel The Lord Our God The Lord Is One." There is also a cornerstone that reads "Congregation Emanu-El 1916 1956" with the corresponding Hebrew dates. This shows that the congregation began elsewhere and moved here in the 1950s. The American Synagogue Directory of 1960 lists Rabbi Aaron H. Blumenthal and President Louis H. Shereff as their leaders.

*Sinai Temple*
*127 Crary Avenue | 10550*

The primary section of this former synagogue is a beautiful, sandy brick building that looks rather like a sizable European villa. The main entrance is framed by two pretty columns, each resembling candle holders with their elaborate upper sections. The decorative segment above the main entrance features a prominent Decalogue in Hebrew. A cornerstone here reads "5687 SINAI TEMPLE". The additional building is plainer in design and has a cornerstone that reads "5719 1958" and the year rendered in Hebrew letters. A church now occupies this campus. Sinai Temple merged with other congregations nearby so it does live on.

*Congregation Brothers of Israel*
*116 Crary Avenue | 10550*

This mottled reddish brick building has a stately style and looks like a nice residence. The exterior Judaica has all been removed. A church is here now. The Google Maps image from October 2007 shows that the synagogue name was still spelled out near the top, and a Jewish star was displayed just below the peak of the roof. The building was a church prior to being a shul.

*Congregation Brothers of Israel*
*10 South 8th Avenue | 10550*

"CBI" had moved from South 8th Avenue to the site at 116 Crary Avenue, in 1980.

The South 8th Avenue building is still quite impressive. The main entrance is highly detailed and in Hebrew it still reads "Beit Haknesset B'nai Israel." A stained glass half-rose window inside this arch has a Jewish star and the quote from Psalms *Zeh Hashaar* although part of it is missing. There are small but noticeable menorah designs in each of the four columns, and many stones on the front have flora and fauna designs. This large, sandy brick building dominates a largely residential block. Each side has four large stained glass windows which are also beautiful: each features a Jewish star and heavenly elements, as well as winged animals and memorial sections. This is a well-maintained building and except for a modest sign from the church, it still looks much like an active synagogue. According to the American Synagogue Directory of 1960, their leaders were Rabbi Solomon Frelich and President Morris Newman.

*Jewish Center of Mount Vernon*
*230 South Columbus Avenue | 10553*

The one obvious Judaic detail to this brick building, now used as a church, is the Decalogue that rises above the roofline. Although it was painted over, it still appears to be a synagogue-like item. Another interesting feature of the front of the building is the set of seven identical windows in a line, above the large main entrance with its arch. We learn from the American Synagogue Directory of 1960 that they were led by Rabbi Joseph H. Wise and President B. Sol Goldfinger.

## YONKERS

*Lincoln Park Jewish Center*
*311 Central Park Avenue | 10704*

This congregation, a Modern Orthodox, Ashkenazi group, was founded in 1938 but the eclectically styled campus was designed and built later on. It had been struggling but was revitalized in 2017, when it became part of a Brooklyn congregation called Vayetar Yitzchok. But now it is being sold again, with its future uncertain. The main building has many pretty memorial windows and Jewish-themed windows, an interesting menorah sculpture on the exterior and another of The Burning Bush, but the most interesting aspects are the large Decalogues, one with Roman numerals and the other with Hebrew letters. They are in front of a circular section of the building. The front door has two names painted on it, both from Brooklyn (Vayetar Yitzchok and Emunas Hatorah). They still held services in the fall of 2024, but now it is listed on real estate websites.

*Congregation Sons of Israel*
*155 Elliott Avenue | 10705*

At some point in the first half of 2024, this building had its highly detailed and very Judaic entrance removed. Even the Google Maps picture from January 2024 shows a Jewish star, Hebrew words, a Decalogue and other details. By the time I showed up in August 2024, that entrance was bricked over. The gate with the synagogue name and two small Jewish stars still remained, as well as a cornerstone that read "Congregation Sons of Israel" and the Hebrew year on one side, "5689" and a Jewish star on the other side. The congregation moved to another location within Yonkers. I had been here several years earlier and seen the previous Judaica. In the American Synagogue Directory of 1960 their leaders are listed as Rabbi Moses S. Malinowitz and President William Levine.

*Temple Emanu-El*
*306 Rumsey Road | 10705*

This mid-century modern set of buildings that used to be Temple Emanu-El still has many stained glass windows from the days of the temple. The taller main building has them intact. There are some other interesting elements to this building which is essentially a box.

The American Synagogue Directory of 1960 states that their rabbi was Dr. Abraham J. Klausner and President Henry H. Renard. They have since merged with a Scarsdale congregation.

## WHITE PLAINS

*Hebrew Institute of White Plains*
*65 Fisher Avenue | 10606*

This modest-sized former synagogue, similar in size and shape to the houses on this block, is a pretty brown brick building with some touches of Judaica remaining. There is a Twelve Tribes motif that flocks the main entrance, six rectangles on each side. There is another stained glass adornment above the entrance. The congregation moved in 1950 to another location in the city.

Congregation Agudath Sholom Jersey City, NJ

Beth El Jacob Albany, NY

Anshe Ticktin Chicago, IL

Anshe Emeth South River, NJ

B'nai Israel Toledo, OH

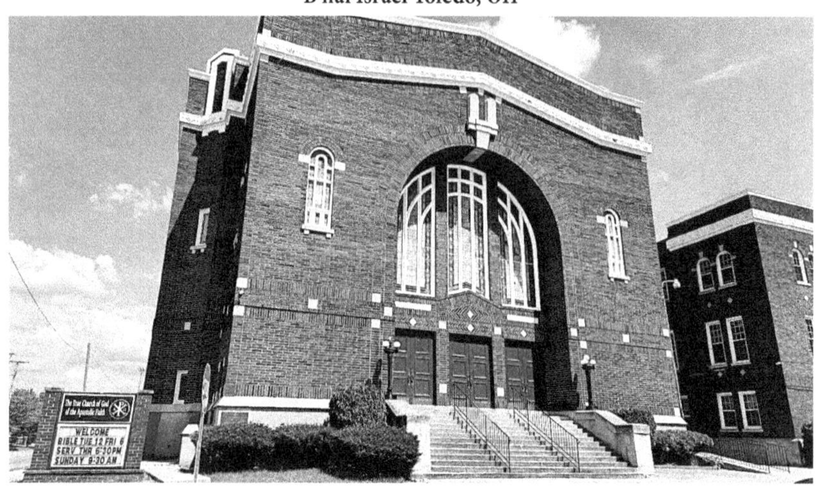


B'nai Jeshurun Philadelphia, PA

B'nai Moshe Detroit, MI

Beth Hamedrash Hagadol Chicago, IL

Ohel Yitzhok Brooklyn, NY

Mishkan Yisroel Detroit, MI

Jewish Center of Pelham Bay Bronx, NY

North Shore Congregation Chicago, IL

Euclid Avenue Temple Cleveland, OH

Cleveland Jewish Center Cleveland, OH

Beth Hamedrash Hagadol Hartford, CT

Agudath Sholom Stamford, CT

Temple Anshe Hesed Erie, PA

B'nai Israel Mt. Vernon, NY

**Temple Beth Emeth Albany, NY**

**Adas Yisroel Passaic, NJ**

Temple Emanuel Paterson, NJ

Beth Uziel Congregation Philadelphia, PA

Temple B'nai David San Francisco, CA

Shaarey Zedek Detroit, MI

## Sharon/Shearith Israel Baltimore, MD

# Former New Jersey Synagogues

I HAVE MADE SEVERAL trips to cities and towns in New Jersey in order to document former synagogues. Living in Brooklyn, it is not difficult for me to venture by car into New Jersey, and it was the first state after New York where I made comprehensive studies. From 2013 onward, after the publication of The Lost Synagogues of Manhattan, I decided to explore urban and then suburban sections of NJ.

I began with Newark (which I have since documented at least five times, including 2022) and areas nearby such as Irvington and East Orange. Later I went to Camden twice, with information gleaned partly from my sister in law's late husband Dean and his brother Fred, natives of Camden. Sometime in 2015 I drove to New Brunswick to document a synagogue that had a devastating fire (now only the front of the building remains; it was redeveloped into housing), and around that time I also drove to Perth Amboy, Hoboken, Asbury Park and later on Atlantic City, in search of former synagogues. (Unfortunately I lost some of that material.)

A particularly helpful and thorough examination of Newark's former synagogues was held at The Jewish Museum of New Jersey, located in the shul building of Ahavas Sholom, the main active synagogue in Newark. In fact, I assisted in conducting part of the research, and attended the opening of this wonderful exhibition in November 2016.

In October 2023 I visited Jersey City and Bayonne to see a few lost synagogues; I revisited a few in Perth Amboy in early January 2024 when I learned that a holdout synagogue had been sold to a church. In November and December 2024 I revisited some sites in Passaic, Paterson, Newark, Jersey City and nearby areas. (I also got rerouted and confused in Passaic when the local high school held a fire drill.)

I have noticed certain similarities between modest and medium-sized urban former synagogue buildings in Newark, Hoboken and Passaic, for example, and many found in Manhattan, Brooklyn and the Bronx. Newark is of particular importance; it was a significant Jewish community for several decades. The situation changed dramatically in the mid-1960s. The fortunes of Newark have fallen and risen, similar to other major American cities.

## NEWARK

*Congregation Ahavath Israel*
*209 Wainwright Street (near Lyons Ave) | 07112*

Basically a boxy building, this site is somewhat remarkable for its mottled orangey brick and its interesting front. It has a variation of the "open Torah front," the two outer sections set forward slightly and the center set back. The first time I stopped by here the name was still visible in Hebrew, but now a church sign covers it. There is still a Decalogue with Hebrew writing and two small Jewish stars. On the side closer to Lyons Avenue you can see stained glass memorial windows. The former Ahavath Israel is walking distance from a few other former shuls. Rabbi Mordecai (Max) Ehrenkrantz was one of the spiritual leaders, and their president according to the American Synagogue Directory of 1960 was Samuel Gershon.

*Adas Israel-Mishnayos*
*246 Shephard Avenue (at Schuyler Avenue) | 07112*

This mottled brown brick corner building has one particularly interesting piece of Judaica: a combination Jewish star-Decalogue at the roofline, above the main entrance. There are several stained glass memorial windows on both sides of the building, and they appear to be from the days of the synagogue. This congregation was located from 1911 to 1939 in the original Oheb Shalom location on Prince Street, an example of what I call "hopscotching" (a congregation vacates and another comes in).

*Ahavath Zion/Uptown Hebrew School*
*148 16th Avenue (at Holland Street) | 07103*

This is a grand, neo-classical building that is situated on a street that comes to a point. The avenue and the street meet at a point, and the building is set back slightly. There is a great deal of visible Judaica here: it reads

Congregation Ahavath Israel in English, with a Jewish star just above it, over the main entrance. An unusual decoration is the open book with Hebrew writing, flanked by the English quotes "God Will Give Strength To His People" on the left and "Call Upon Him While He Is Near" on the right. Each of the three front doors has a Jewish star above it. On the 16th Avenue side, toward the back, it says "V'Uptown TT" in phonetic Hebrew, and below in English it says "Uptown Hebrew School." Toward the front of the building there is a "1921" cornerstone with some fading Hebrew writing on one side. The building has other pleasant decorative touches. From the American Synagogue Directory of 1960 we learn that Rabbi Sholom B. Gordon and President Jack Weber led the congregation. Previous rabbis (or "reverends") include Louis Zapeikov and Max Radin, from 1923–1934.

*Ahavas Achim B'nai Jacob/Tzemach Tzedek*
*391 Avon Avenue (at South 13th Street) | 07103*

This boxy brick corner former synagogue has two Decalogues with Hebrew writing one on each exposed side of the building. There are three Jewish stars near the roofline, two just above the main doors, and two on the doors themselves. The American Synagogue Directory of 1960 lists Rabbi Hershel Cohen and President Morris I. Miller as their leaders. The website for the still-active "AABJ" tells us that Tzemach Tzedek began in the 1920s and the cornerstone was laid in 1937, but they had financial problems and were absorbed by Anshe Lemberg B'nai Jacob; together known as B'nai Jacob. But with the population changes in Newark, they relocated to the suburbs in the 1960s.

*B'nai Abraham*
*621 Clinton Avenue (between Shanley Avenue and South 10th St) | 07108*

This is a large and unusually designed former synagogue, notable for its large domed roof and two entrances, each stately. Between the two entrances, on the Clinton side, are four large columns, a set of beautiful stained glass windows, and the name Temple B'nai Abraham in English, but the word "Temple" is in good shape while the other two are shoddier. From the American Synagogue Directory of 1960 we learn that the rabbi then was Dr. Joachim Prinz, rather well known, and their president was Norman Feldman. Prinz wrote several books and was heavily involved in both pro-Israel and pro-civil rights activities. The congregation actually began in the 1850s; this building was their home from 1924 to 1973, and was designed by Nathan Myers. Later it became a Pentecostal church and then a charter school. The congregation relocated to Livingston. The building is on the National Register of Historic Places.

*Congregation Anshe Russia*
*224 West Kinney Street (at Prince Street) | 07103*

This site has to be scrutinized in order to see that it does indeed have remaining Judaica. Above the trio of front doors, and the sign for the church residing there now, you can spot the ghosting of Hebrew letters in two locations. This building is a pleasant-looking site of red brick and cast stone, and looks quite like a school or library. Their spiritual leaders included Reverend Hyman Brodsky, Reverend Joseph Konvitz, and Reverend Koolyk. An article from late 1900 noted that the building cost around $30,000 to build. Another news article from 1907 noted that the congregation was "largely made up of Russians and Roumanians." It featured a photograph of the choir, which is praised highly in the article.

*Oheb Shalom*
*32 Prince Street (near South Orange Avenue) | 07103*

Here is a gem of a building, artistically and historically, and Newark should be applauded for preserving, renovating and giving it a worthy reuse as an outdoor learning center. This red brick building has various pretty details, with keyhole windows as well as a lovely rose window above the entrance. Look to the roofline to see small, pretty Jewish stars. Glance at the left of the entrance for the original stone sign that reads in Hebrew "Bet HaKnesset Adat Israel".(Also spot the historic signs placed later on.) The back section is the modern part of the urban environmental center and while it doesn't quite match the original building, it is attractive and fits in. This is the second oldest Jewish congregation in Newark and the building was used from 1860–1911.

*B'nai Jeshurun*

*785 MLK Jr Blvd/High St (at Muhammad Ali Avenue) | 07108*

The first time I visited this grand complex, which had been a home of Newark's oldest Jewish congregation, it was being used as a church; I was able to get inside because I arrived shortly before a funeral service commenced. A kind congregant allowed me to snap photos quickly in the main sanctuary, and then in the outer sections.The next time I showed up, a few years later, the church was gone and it was being renovated into an events space. How intriguing that a synagogue became a church, Hopewell Baptist Church, and was then turned into a secular space.

This has long been a most impressive building, and so much remains to be ogled. The architect was Albert S. Gottlieb. The dome, inside and out, is fabulous. There are several gorgeous stained glass windows with memorial segments. Look around and you can see various Judaic symbols, from menorahs to Jewish stars, and look carefully outside for a chiseled Hebrew-English dedication that reads "God Will Give Strength To His People" from Psalms, paired with 1848–1914. Rabbi Ely E.Pilchik was their spiritual leader according to the American Synagogue Directory of 1960; that book also listed 17 Waverly Avenue as the address, the side street, instead of what was then High Street. They moved in 1968 to Short Hills and then the church moved in for many years. The building was being renovated in the 2020s by the Matiteebs, a Jewish father-son firm.

*Oheb Shalom*
*672 MLK Jr Blvd/High St | 07102*

This was the next home for Oheb Shalom, after Prince Street. Spacious open lots surround this former synagogue on both sides; whatever buildings were precisely adjacent are gone. But the old YM-YWHA still anchors the corner, and these two buildings make an impressive pair, on what has long been a prominent block in this section of Newark. This building retains Judaica, such as a Jewish star in a pediment above the main entrance, and a four-word Hebrew phrase that comes from Psalms and is sung during the processional for returning Torah scrolls to the Holy Ark, on Shabbat (*Hishtahavu L'Adonai B'hadrat Kodesh*). Those are not the typical words that I have seen engraved on synagogues, active or lost. There are also several pretty stained glass windows remaining from the synagogue days. This is a pretty building, now occupied by a church. This neo-classical building does not resemble the earlier Oheb Shalom, but both are wonderful structures.

The congregation resided here from 1911–1958. Rabbi Charles Hoffman was the first to helm the pulpit here, and the early cantors were Max Helfere and then Moses Gann. Later Edgar Mills was the cantor. Later the congregation moved to suburban West Orange.

*Old YM-YWHA*
*652 MLK Jr Blvd/High St (at West Kinney Street) | 07102*

This stately corner building is the next-door neighbor to the former Oheb Shalom, and the two make a nice, neo-classical pairing. Look for the cornerstone that reads "1922" and ponder that this building has passed the 100 year mark. There are many pretty details on this brick and stone building, but I only found one Jewish star remaining. Two of the original benefactors of the Y were Louis Bamberger and Felix Fuld. The building appears to be in nice shape but needs a power washing. The building was sold in 1955 to an African American group, and the Y moved to the Weequahic neighborhood, on Chancellor Avenue.

*Toras Emes*
*79 Jefferson Street | 07105*

This former synagogue, "the Ferry Street shul," was located in the Ironbound section of Newark, which did not have as great a concentration of Jews as other areas such as Weequahic. It is an interesting-looking building, and now a church. Two small Jewish stars are still visible near the tops of columns flanking the main entrance. A cornerstone is chiseled with "Aug. 22, 1909."

President Isidore Rems is listed in the American Synagogue Directory of 1960. This congregation was later absorbed into AABJD in West Orange.

*Ahavath Achim B'nai Israel*
*706 Nye Avenue | Irvington | 07111*

At this point a rather plain, boxy building, there are a few intriguing clues to its past. You can see the backs of memorial windows on the sides of the structure, and there is an interesting decorative pattern with circles on the front above the entrance. (According to Google Maps, this was altered sometime after 2018.) The brick back section of the building has hints of remaining and/or removed Judaica. Rabbi Benjamin H. Englander and President Horace Bier are listed in the American Synagogue Directory of 1960. Referred to as one of the "alphabet shuls" in Irvington, it merged with the Chancellor Avenue synagogue in the late 1970s. The merged congregation sold this Nye Avenue site in the early 1990s, and moved to be with Beth Shalom in Union.

*Agudath (Ahavath) Achim Bickur Cholim*
*642 Chancellor Avenue | Irvington | 07111*

This sandy brick building sits solidly on a corner of land, with four streamlined columns in front of the main entrance. Look carefully near the top of each column to spy faded Jewish stars.

The American Synagogue Directory of 1960 lists Rabbi Leon J. Yagod and President Wolf Teltser as their leaders. Cantor Jack Korbman was the hazzan for many years. In the back of the sanctuary, there was a plaque in honor of a bar mitzvah boy named Jerry Levitch– better known to the world as Jerry Lewis. This congregation then moved into the Nye Avenue building (above).

*Zichron Moshe (?)*
*929 Bergen Street | 07112*

This is a modest, boxy former synagogue with a few quaint touches and some slightly hidden Judaica. If you look carefully at the circular window that is partially obscured by the church sign, you can see a Jewish star of stained glass. Easier to see is the Decalogue which seems to have missing details. This area had been heavily Jewish up through the early 1960s.

## JERSEY CITY

*Congregation Agudath Sholom*
*472 Bergen Avenue (near Clinton Avenue) | 07304*

This former synagogue has been a church for decades, but it still presents more as a Jewish house of worship, due to the abundance of remaining Judaica on the exterior. In fact, the only major reminder that it is Christian is the church name, painted on the trio of arches at the front entrance.

There is a pair of towers, one on each side, each topped with a dome and multiple Jewish stars. There are three free-standing Jewish stars, one atop each tower and one at the peak of the entrance roofline. There are a few other Jewish star medallions on the front, and a trapezoidal staircase, the type that can be seen on many other synagogues from the early 1900s in other locales including New York City. The building does have some wear and tear. According to the American Synagogue Directory of 1960 their leaders were Rabbi C. Levene and President Robert Wasserman.

*United Sons of Bikur Cholim*
*37 Wayne Street (near Grove Street) | 07302*

This off-white brick building is dingy and shows fraying at the edges, but there are two stained glass windows with one Jewish star in each window. These appear to be the sole remains of the former synagogue. It was originally built in 1852 as a church, then was a synagogue in 1923 until the early 1950s. After that a few other churches moved in and out of the structure. It is being turned into housing, with much of the original external design being retained.

*Grove Street Synagogue*
*295 Grove Street (near Wayne Street) | 07302*

This former Orthodox synagogue, midblock on a busy downtown street, has a pretty front full of Judaica. It has been used as a mosque for several years, and the Muslim congregation removed two cherished pieces of Judaica, the two cast stone Lions of Judah from above the main entrance, sometime after 2016 according to Google Maps. But there are still two Jewish stars near the roofline and a small Decalogue in the middle. There are multiple stained glass windows from the shul days, with four menorah designs visible. One time in the mid-2010s I visited inside the building and saw other stained glass memorial windows remaining from the synagogue days. (It was a Friday, so I removed my sandals, as per the mosque requirements. But congregants were okay with my taking photographs of the memorabilia inside.)

*Congregation Ohab Sholom Hebrew Institute*
*126 Rutgers Avenue at Stevens Avenue | 07305*

This red-white brick building has a nice corner garden and now houses a church, but there is still a bit of Judaica visible on the exterior: a cast-stone Jewish star near the roofline. A few windows were bricked over and others covered with thick red glass. The American Synagogue Directory of 1960 lists Rabbi Isaac Siegal and President Harry Hittner as their leaders.

*Congregation Tifereth Israel*
*238 5th Street | 07302*

This looks like a pretty, subdued private home in the middle of a residential block, but there are attractive stained glass windows on the front and sides. Three of those windows that flank the main entrance are memorial windows from the synagogue, and each has a prominent Jewish star. The building may have originally served as a church, then became a shul, and then in the 1980s became residences. The StreetEasy real estate website mentions it was built in 1889.

*Bergen Hebrew Institute*
*2 Oxford Avenue at Sackett Street | 07304*

This stately brown-brick building was and still is used as a school, and there is quite a bit of Judaica still visible on the exterior. Above the main entrance you can see "BERGEN INSTITUTE" and there are different types of small Jewish stars near the roofline, a few flat and a few placed inside concrete medallions. Perhaps the most unique Judaica pieces are found on the iron gate surrounding the building: a set of Jewish stars with BB inside each one (and they cast pretty shadows). One cornerstone reads in Hebrew "Talmud Torah Agudath Sholom" with the Hebrew date. Another cornerstone by Sackett Street is in English and reads "Bergen Hebrew Institute" with the Jewish year, but it's hard to decipher. From the sidewalk you can see the tower and dome of the former Agudath Sholom at 472 Bergen Avenue.

*Sherman Avenue Talmud Torah*
*100 Sherman Avenue | 07307*

This brown-brick building has some nice decorative touches and at least two pieces of Judaica still visible on the front: way at the top of the roof there is a decorative medallion with a small decalogue inside it, and a cornerstone on the right-hand side of the building is in Hebrew, with numbers arrayed around a Jewish star. "5673" and "1913," as well the Hebrew year rendered in Hebrew letters, can be seen as well as two *Tof* letters, which stand for Talmud Torah.

## BAYONNE

*Ohab Sholem*
*1014 Avenue C (near West 49th Street) | 07002*

The former Ohab Sholem building, along with the next door Hebrew school building, are a pairing that reflects Bayonne's Jewish past. The synagogue building is quite nice; an orange brick building with remaining Judaica such as a Decalogue with Hebrew, at the very top of the entrance area, a pretty rose window with stained glass and a Jewish star, and other stained glass windows (some of which are not in good condition). There is also a brass plaque on the street level with both Hebrew and English texts. An interesting element to the front of the building is the way the brick sections alternate between recessed and extended, giving the exterior more depth. The school building is plainer, and the cast stone signs near the roofline were mostly scraped out or deteriorated, except for one where you can discern the faint words "Talmud Torah" and others words. The synagogue was founded in 1915 and the school was built in 1928. The American Synagogue Directory of 1960 lists their rabbi as Ruben H. Bendelstein and their president as I. Leibowitz.

## SOUTH RIVER

*Anshe Emeth*
*88 Main Street (near Gordon Street) | South River*

This boxy, ranch style brick building is now a Latino church but had been a synagogue called Anshe Emeth. The most obvious piece of remaining Judaica is a seven-branched menorah to the right of the main doors, and this set above a cast-stone plaque that reads "Great is Truth and Mighty Above

All Things." Also near the door, but less noticeable, is a cornerstone reading "1952/5712". When I peeped inside the main entrance I also noticed a Jewish star on a wall in the main corridor. There are a few stained glass windows that seem to be from the synagogue days, including one above the main doors that resembles a menorah. In the American Synagogue Directory of 1960 their leaders were listed as Rabbi Joseph Maza and President Abe S. Schwartz. The congregation actually began in 1916, and merged with Highland Park Conservative Temple.

## PASSAIC

*Adas Yisroel/Tulip Street Shul*
*11 Tulip Street | 07055*

I have stopped by the former Adas Yisroel, the Tulip Street Shul, on a few occasions and each time have noted that it's a little gem of a building. Its size and overall design are modest, but the various details and decorative touches are pretty and well maintained. You will see attractive windows, stained glass memorial plaques, a few Jewish stars and neat brickwork. From the Montgomery Street side you can see a small archway with a Jewish star and other nice details.

The building was erected in 1928 although the congregation was actually founded in 1921. It started out as a one-story building but was expanded upward. In 1969 the building was closed and sold; now it is used as a church. The congregation moved elsewhere within Passaic, to 565 Broadway. Rutgers University has partial archival holdings.

*B'nai Jacob*
*112 Washington Place | 07055*

The handsome, neat brick building that you can still see on Washington Place replaced a wooden structure that burnt down. It cost $130,000 to build, and the rabbi serving then was Rev. Jacob L. Katain. Rutgers University has its archival holdings. President David Minsky is listed in the American Synagogue Directory of 1960. A carved sign near the roofline reads "Congregation of B'nai Jacob." The cornerstone features the secular year "1927" and there are other, smaller words in Hebrew. I visited inside once and at the time (around 2014 or 2015) there were a few pieces of

Judaica inside. In the September 2008 Google Maps photo, you can still see a sizable carved Jewish star just below the roofline. It has since been covered up by signs placed there by first one and then another church.

## PATERSON

*Temple Emanuel*
*Broadway and East 33rd Street | 07514*

This building was a gorgeous structure in its heyday, and was designed by Frederick W. Wentworth. It was completed in 1929. Jacob Fabian, the congregational president, donated the funds for the construction of this Conservative temple. There is even a silent film of the groundbreaking ceremony. Even in a disheveled state, this Art Deco building with its many fantastic details, ranging from painted designs to carvings, and even elaborate door handles, is a treasure. But the majority of the stained glass windows were removed to the current version of Temple Emanuel, and the beautiful main sanctuary skylight is falling apart. The former school building is on the East 33rd Street side. The American Synagogue Directory of 1960 lists Rabbi Arthur T. Buch and President Gerrard Berman as their leaders. But by the 1970s the congregation was diminishing and in the 1980s it merged with Oakland Jewish Community Center. They relocated to Franklin Lakes, a suburb.

## PERTH AMBOY

*Beth Mordecai*
*224 High Street | 08861*

This is a sizable, nice-looking former synagogue that is largely faced in sandy colored brick. There is a Decalogue at the roofline, and a pretty rose window. A cornerstone reads "1926" in English, and the Hebrew date is there as well. The scalloping design near the top is similar in style to some former synagogues in Brooklyn. Rabbi Max D. Davidson and President Moses M. Eisemann are listed as their leaders in the American Synagogue Directory of 1960. According to their Facebook page, on March 13, 2022, the congregation held a Deconsecration ceremony here. Photos and text accompany the announcement.. The congregation said they made the decision to close up and sell the building because they could not afford to maintain it. It is quite sad, but by documenting they showed how this kind of mournful event is performed.

*Shaarey Tefiloh*
*15 Market Street | 08861*

This boxy, sprawling corner building, faced in stone, still displayed the synagogue name in Hebrew and English in September 2012, according to a Google Maps photo. Now it shows two small reminders of the shul: a small stone that reads "Oct. 4, 1903" and another that reads "November 1976" and "Kislev" in Hebrew with the Jewish year. Their previous address, according to the American Synagogue Directory of 1960, was 314 Madison Avenue. At that time their rabbi was Simcha Levy and their president was Abraham Weinstein. Now a different religious group resides at 15 Market Street.

## NEW BRUNSWICK

*Poile Zedek*
*145 Neilson Street | 08901*

There is a modern, upscale residence in New Brunswick called the Lofts at Neilson Crossing. Curiously, the front resembles an old synagogue– because from the early 1920s onward, it was known as Poile Zedek, an Orthodox Jewish congregation. You can still see the shul name in English, above the entrance, and a Jewish star ornament at the peak of the roof. In October 2015 the building sustained a huge fire. I heard about this on the news and visited it, to see the remains. It is interesting and heartening to see that part of the building has remained visible. The congregation actually began in 1901.

# Former Synagogues in Philadelphia and Allentown

In the northeastern section of the United States, after New York City, there is no other city that has as many former synagogues and schools still standing as does Philadelphia. Driving around and visiting these many sites, I was struck by certain similarities these buildings shared with former synagogues throughout New York City, and to some extent as well with urban New Jersey, particularly Newark and Jersey City. There are various differences as well, but the dense concentration in certain areas is similar to what can be found in parts of Brooklyn, the East Village of Manhattan and the Bronx, in particular.

One marked feature of some Philadelphia former synagogues is their location on rather narrow streets. Size-wise, the lost synagogues of Philadelphia are a mixed group: some are modest, located on busy urban streets. Others are more expansive and have a suburban style and layout. They run the gamut of styles. Many have been turned into churches but others have been repurposed in different ways.

I have visited Philadelphia several times during my lifetime, but the three trips I took in the summer of 2023 and one in 2024 were important to my study of the city's former synagogues. By combing through the 1960 American Jewish Yearbook and looking at Facebook pages devoted to the old Jewish community, I was able to gather together several names and addresses. It is not too long a drive from Brooklyn, so I was able to make day trips.

*Adath Shalom/Beth Shmuel*
*2400 South Marshall Street (607 West Ritner Street) | 19148*

There are two intriguing elements at this former synagogue on a corner: one is the pretty Decalogue with Hebrew writing, above the doors, and the other is a decorative piece above the door, attached to the brick. It's not clear if that piece is from the synagogue or was an initiative of the church that is there now. There are a few stylistic touches that are reminiscent of streamlined Art Deco, and some modifications were made over time, noticeable where the brick color is slightly different. They started out as Beth Shmuel in 1922. In 1950 it became a Conservative synagogue, with the merger of two other congregations into the site. Among the rabbis who served there were Aaron Decter, Robert Tabak, and Gail Glickman, who was their final rabbi. Officially the shul closed in 2007, and certain religious pieces were given to Congregation Tiferes B'nai Israel in Warrington, PA. This building housed a Buddhist temple for a while, and then became a Latino church.

*Beth El/Rothschild Memorial Synagogue*
*137 South 58th Street (at Walnut Street) | 19139*

Anchored on a corner, this large former synagogue has some very impressive features. There are three arched doors, each topped by a very pretty, intricate mosaic of sorts, with Hebrew words, fruits, and multiple Jewish stars woven together. The middle door piece shows a Decalogue and the Revelation at Mount Sinai. Above this is a lengthy memorial dedication, and at the corner of the building is a small cornerstone for Congregation Beth El. This is a beautiful, memorable building with a stone facing. According to a Philadelphia Inquirer article from September 6, 1915, "Rothschild Memorial Synagogue Dedicated," "Officers of the congregation, bearing the sacred scrolls, marched around the synagogue after the cantor had intoned an appropriate passage of the Scriptures." A community center was added to the synagogue in 1922. The architect for the building was Louis Levi. The congregation later merged with Beth Hillel and relocated to Wynnewood.

*B'nai Jeshurun*
*2117 North 33rd Street (near West Diamond Street) | 19121*

From the front this appears to have been a sizable former synagogue, but it's actually much bigger. It extends back to North Douglas Street, and that side of the campus is much shabbier. The front of the main building is pretty, a mottled stone facing. The main entrance is dramatic, with a sculpted combination of a Jewish star and menorah window, detailed pilasters, fruit and floral motifs, and more, with the church's cross in front of it all, a bit awkwardly. A small box of a building obscures more of the windows, some with ogee designs on top. Hess and Sugarman designed the building. According to the American Synagogue Directory of 1960, Rabbi Marshall J. Maltzman and President Albert M. Cohen were their leaders. This was a Conservative congregation. Other rabbis here were Max Drob and Joseph Zeitlin.

*Beth Judah*
*5426 Sansom Street | 19139*

This pretty, modest-sized former synagogue is interesting primarily because it is set back far from the sidewalk, and it has a beautiful floral rose window. The dome is also quite nice. The Judaica left here consists of two Jewish stars on the gate at the sidewalk. There are several other well-kept stained glass windows as well. This building has similarities to a former synagogue in Williamsburg, Brooklyn and a few others, with this particular layout.

It was an Orthodox congregation, established in 1905 and chartered in 1908; it disbanded in 1968. The American Synagogue Directory of 1960 mentions Rabbi Solomon Shoulson and President Albert Goldberg. In 1989 this congregation merged into Shaare Shamayim, along with other defunct groups. At least once they held a Shabbat service for Shomrim, the Jewish police officers fraternal group.

*Beth Hamedrash Hagadol*
*6029 Larchwood Avenue | 19143*

This medium-sized, mottled brown brick building may have a cross attached to it, but it also has several Jewish stars in nicely-kept stained glass windows, and the name Beth Hamedrash Hagaold stamped in Hebrew, in an arch above the main door. Overall it is a streamlined building with neat brick designs. It closed around 1990. Two blocks away at 5934 Larchwood Avenue was the former Lenas HaZedek, a corner building that no longer shows any Judaica on the exterior.

*Anshe Sfard*
*3011 West Cumberland Street (at North Corlies Street) | 19132*

One of the more modest former synagogues of Philadelphia, this corner building has a milky blue, stained-glass Jewish star at the front door and a small cornerstone that reads "Rebuilt Aug. 10, 1926." That kind of very specific detail is not typical of a cornerstone; it tells part of a story. The church there now put up a cross and a brick cross near the roofline.

*Har Zion*
*2251 North 54th Street (at Woodcrest Avenue) | 19131*

The old building does not seem to have any remaining Judaica on the exterior, but the newer, boxy brick building (which is also much larger) has many pretty stained glass windows that can be seen easily even from outside. The shul was chartered in 1923 and their first rabbi was Simon Greenberg. The American Synagogue Directory of 1960 lists their leaders as Rabbi David A. Goldstein and President Hyman Bomze. Mr. Bomze was a dress manufacturer who died in October 1966, according to his obituary listing in the Philadelphia Daily News. This Conservative congregation moved to the Penn Valley area and is still active.

*Anshe Sode Loden*
*501 Mercy Street (near South 5th Street) | 19148*

This unassuming row house of red brick has one intriguing clue to its past: a faded sign with a Jewish star. If you scrutinize the sign more, you will see the ghosting of Hebrew letters as well. The sign appears to have been painted over multiple times, but the Jewish essence somehow peeks through. Then you will notice the two sets of six small dedication stones/bricks by the first floor window, all with Hebrew. Very interesting find.

*Fastover Congregation*
*599 Sigel Street/1826 South 6th Street | 19148*

What essentially looks like a bland, pale-orange brick corner building has some interesting pieces of Judaica. There is a cornerstone that gives a mini-history of the group: "Ind. Fastover Cong. Organized 1916 Rebuilt 1951 Jack L. Leba" and part of the last name is a bit scratched out. On the upper level of the building there is a plaque, painted white, with Hebrew and English: Fastover written in Hebrew/Yiddish and English, along with a pretty design of a Decalogue, two Lions of Judah, a crown, along with a Jewish star and a menorah. This charming decoration is a bit different from those gracing synagogues that I have seen throughout the United States. It is compact and pretty.

*Berditchev Congregation*
*604 Dickinson Street (at South Marshall Street) | 19147*

This brick building is from 1896, and there is a little cornerstone, painted black, that mentions this. The style is somewhat different than many other former synagogues that date to the early 1900s. It has several pretty lancet windows with arches and neat brickwork. Certain elements seem to have been spackled and painted over, particularly near the peak of the roof, leading me to think there was Judaica there previously.

*B'nai Reuben*
*615 South 6th Street (at Kater Street) | 19147*

This delightful corner building is basically a box, but it has a beautiful entrance and many attractive decorative elements throughout the front and side of the building. There are two pieces of the Jewish past here: the gate at the alley has pretty scrolling within which can be found a Jewish star, and there is a small cornerstone that reads "May 22 1904". Up until at least June 2014, according to Google Maps, there were also two Jewish stars on the front of the building on the ground floor level, with Hebrew words inside each. Over the entrance in narrow Hebrew lettering there was the name of the congregation, Bet Haknesset B'nai Ruvin with the designation of Anshe Sfard. In addition there were two circular medallions that split a famous line from the psalms that make up part of the Hallel prayer service. *(Ze hashaar)*

The very narrow Fairhill Street is the back border of the building, really more of an alley. The congregation left the building in 1956. It served as an antiques shop for a while and is now condominiums.

*B'nai Halbershtam*
*619 North 6th Street | 19147*

This nice-looking orange brick building has a trio of doors, pretty stained glass windows on either side of the building, and a Jewish star motif in blue and white, near the roofline above the entrance. The brickwork was done in a clever manner so as to achieve a deeper look.

North 6th St was the home of B'nai Halberstam from 1895–1960. It was one of the many shuls in this part of immigrant Jewish Philadelphia, the area around Marshall Street. It merged at least twice with other congregations as time went on, and still exists today, in another location.

*Ohel Jacob*
*1717 North 7th Street (near Cecil B. Moore Avenue) | 19122*

This is one of the more unusual former synagogues in Philadelphia, and it is a delight to gaze upon. A church had been here for many years but when I visited it in the summer of 2023, it was gone and renovation was being done. This building features windows of the "Rundbogenstil" style, the rounded "keyhole" look. There is also an unusual design on the front, with six smaller windows surrounding one in the middle, within one bigger circle (it looks like a cartridge of some type). A sign above the doorway, etched in Hebrew and English, reads "K.K. Ohel Yakov Congregation Ohel Jacob Ellul 17 5671 September 10 1911." A Hidden City article of 2012 points out that it was built in 1888 as a different synagogue, Adath Yeshurun Congregation. There was even a Jewish orphanage on that street. It is a unique building in several aspects, and there are many other pleasing details throughout the front and some on the side of the building.

*Beth Hamidrash Hagadol*
*2838 Tulip Street (at East Auburn Street) | 19134*

This is a medium-sized corner building, now a church, that has one remnant of its former Jewish life: a cornerstone with stylized Hebrew letters that reads "Bet Hamedrash Hagadol" and the date in Hebrew. It looks as if someone scribbled graffiti on it at some point. This shul has been listed as part of the Jew Town neighborhood.

*Achduth B'nei Israel*
*540 West Erie Street | 19140*

This former synagogue of brownish brick looks small from the front, but it does extend back pretty far. It has a rather plain style but it does resemble many other urban former synagogues that need to maximize space. There are stained glass windows here that do seem to have been modified from their earlier Jewish styles (and some may have also been broken).

*Congregation Emanu-El*
*6201 Old York Road (at Stenton Avenue) | 19141*

Stop by this building, now a church, and you will see several stained glass windows and stone engravings with Jewish themes such as the Twelve Tribes. The American Synagogue Directory of 1960 lists their leaders as Rabbi Maxwell M. Farber and President Louis Kasoff.

*Temple Sinai*
*2001 East Washington Lane (at Limekiln Pike) | 19138*

This sprawling post WW2 building campus has nice lawns, a bland paint job (it is now a mosque and school, but had been used as a church before) and some of the stained glass windows seem to be from the days of the synagogue. They have abstract patterns that were favored by some other midcentury shul buildings. According to the American Synagogue Directory of 1960 their leader was Rabbi Sidney Greenberg. One of their cantors was Nathan Chaitovsky. The congregation formed in 1942 in a building on Ogontz Avenue. A few years later this building was constructed, and the school building a few years later. They are now located in the suburb of Dresher.

*Agudas Achim*
*625 North 2nd Street | Allentown | 18102*

This smallish former synagogue looks peculiar now because it has an odd staircase. If you know that many synagogues, past and present, have trapezoidal staircases, then you will realize that the old staircase was cut in half. There does not seem to be obvious Judaica here, but that oddity is an identifier. The shul was located here starting in 1893. It was still open in the early 2020s.

*Beth T'fillah*
*2605 Welsh Road | 19114*

This is a boxy, sprawling former synagogue on a corner, with a largely brick exterior. The remaining Judaica on what is now the Eben-Ezer Church of God includes two sizable Jewish stars and a group of seven windows with designs depicting scenes from the Old Testament. Their content focuses on the life of Moses, and comprises an interesting grouping.

I have seen this style of stained glass windows in a few former synagogues in New York City, including at least one in the Bronx and one in Brooklyn. It was built in the early 1950s and has merged more than once with other Philadelphia congregations.

*Beth Emeth*
*Bustleton and Unruh Avenues (6632 SR 1009) | 19149*

The former Beth Emeth is a basic rectangular building, made more interesting for its colored panel windows and a slightly surreal set of windows on the first floor that feature Jewish symbols, such as a menorah, a Torah scroll, and more, woven into a pattern. (These windows have a distinct look similar to those found on the former Sephardic Jewish Center that was on East 169th Street, west of the Grand Concourse.) There is also one remaining Jewish star on the stair railing by the front door entrance. They are listed in the American Synagogue Directory of 1960 with Rabbi Leo Landman and President Jack Schachter. The building dates to 1950.

*Beth Uziel Congregation*
*537 East Wyoming Avenue (at Rorer Street) | 19120*

This synagogue was dedicated in 1954, and in 1994 it closed and merged with Ner Zedek. According to the American Synagogue Directory of 1960 they were helmed by Rabbi Isidore Barnett and President Joseph Shane. Essentially this is a plain brick, boxy corner building, with a few interesting Jewish markers. The entrance by the corner has a cast stone Decalogue with Hebrew letters, and the other entrance beside the houses features a quote from Psalm 100, rendered in large carved Hebrew words and below it a smaller English translation ("Enter Into His Gates With Thanksgiving.") This psalm is recited daily. Also interesting is that the house of worship here now is Jerusalem Seventh Day Adventist Church.

*Beth Sholom*
*4541 North Broad Street (at Courtland Street) | 19140*

This former shul sits majestically on a corner; notice how the streets come to a point, and the way it is set back with a sidewalk plaza in front of it. The congregation was incorporated in 1919 and this building was dedicated in 1921. As stately as this building is, it is overshadowed by its successor site, the famous Elkins Park building designed by Frank Lloyd Wright and built in the late 1950s. Their first rabbi was Mortimer J. Cohen. You can still see small carved Jewish stars of cast stone around the main entrance. A church is here now.

*Beth Jacob*
*6027 Chestnut Street | 19139*

This grayish building has a few clues from its Hebraic past: one cornerstone reads "5707" and another reads "1947." There is also a metal gate that has a Jewish star and the word "Auditorium." It closed in the 1960s and merged with Beth Hamedrash Hagadol. Now a church resides here. This is one of the former synagogues that artist Zoe Cohen painted in watercolors in 2015, for an exhibition about former synagogues in Philadelphia.

*Beth Am Israel*
*5747 Warrington Avenue | 19143*

This was a Conservative synagogue, founded in 1924, and the synagogue building dates to 1926. In 1973 they moved to Penn Valley and the congregation is still there. The American Synagogue Directory of 1960 lists Rabbi Morris S. Goodblatt and President Jack Pearson as their leaders. This stately brown brick building anchors the corner of a largely residential street. The church there now has nicely maintained the building, and there are several original windows remaining with stained glass featuring Jewish stars. The overall style is similar to other 1920s synagogue buildings I have seen in New York City and elsewhere.

# Former Pennsylvania Synagogues

By far, the largest Jewish community in Pennsylvania has been in Philadelphia. Philadelphia also has the biggest number of lost synagogues in the state. But other cities and towns have had their share as well. Pittsburgh and its nearby towns such as Homestead in the southwest, Erie in the northwest, Mount Carmel and Shamokin in central, Allentown in the east: these and other areas are home to former synagogues. I wanted to document major urban sections of the Keystone State and their former synagogues, as well as a few smaller areas.

The former synagogues of Pittsburgh I encountered when I visited the city for a separate writing assignment. In late October 2019 I spent a day and night in Pittsburgh, almost a year after the horrible murders committed at the Tree of Life synagogue in the Squirrel Hill neighborhood. Thus I combined a separate work assignment with my interest in former synagogues, and also paid tribute and homage to the active Jewish community of Pittsburgh.

While in Pittsburgh I documented five former synagogues, a few rather large. I also drove over to Homestead to see the remaining lost shul there, and I went around Squirrel Hill to see the active congregations of the city. The Rauh Jewish Archives are an extremely valuable resource for Pittsburgh Jewish life and synagogues in particular.

I visited Erie in early July 2023, on my way west from Buffalo and onward to Detroit. I drove to the lost synagogues in Shamokin, Mt. Carmel and Allentown in mid-July 2023.

## SHAMOKIN

*B'nai Israel*
*7 East Sunbury Street (near North 8th Street) | 17872*

You might assume this building was still being used as B'nai Israel, if you only saw the name above the entrance and not the church plaque to the left of the entrance, nor the free-standing lawn sign. This modest-sized brick building has an impressive entrance, with neo-classical details. The most striking element is the rose window, of milky stained-glass panels and a Jewish star in the middle. The sides of the building also have pretty stained glass windows. This lovely structure looks out of place amidst the private homes on the street. According to the International Jewish Cemetery Project, this congregation was established on November 23, 1903. There is a corresponding congregational cemetery "with 150 graves on a hill outside of Shamokin." According to the Shamokin News-Dispatch of October 16, 1936, "Benjamin Malett, local merchant, was elected president of the B'nai Israel congregation at a recent election of officers."

A few decades later, the American Synagogue Directory of 1960 listed Rabbi Meyer Horovitz and President Maurice Liachowitz as their leaders.

## MOUNT CARMEL

*Tifereth Israel Mt. Carmel*
*135 South Maple Street (near West 5th Street) | 17851*

This may be a smallish, boxy building of brown brick and modest roofline designs, but the pretty and well-kept stained glass windows reveal the previous life of the synagogue. The front and exposed left side feature lovely windows with Jewish stars and designs. The only obvious signs of its current use as a Masonic Hall are a cornerstone and two signs above the entrance. This overall style is similar to many former and active synagogues throughout New York City, for example. According to their website, the congregation incorporated in August 1896 but didn't build a permanent building of its own until 1922. Eventually the congregation decreased greatly and in April 1986 they sold the building, which now serves as a Masonic Temple. The last bar mitzvah to take place there was in May 1978, for Louis Matlow. The Torah scrolls were sold and other religious items were sold mostly to Jewish institutions.

## ERIE

*Temple Anshe Hesed*
*930 Liberty Street (at West 10th Street) | 16502*

This large, pretty corner building has an eclectic-styled main section with a plainer but still attractive two-story school building. The main building has a castle-like appearance, with a grand arched entrance and three doorways. A Decalogue with Hebrew words is above the doors. One of the more interesting synagogue details that remains is on the school building: "The Currick Memorial: A House of Prayer, A House of Study, A House of Fellowship For All People." Hopefully the Currick family will know about this remaining sign.This Reform congregation has a lengthy history: originally incorporated in May 1862, their first shul building was built in 1882. The building showcased here was dedicated in June 1930, but they have since moved to their current location on Old Zuck Road. They have been led by fourteen rabbis, one of whom was a woman. According to the American Synagogue Directory of 1960, Rabbi Randall M. Falk and President Arthur G. Ostheim led the congregation. According to Marta Braiterman Tanenbaum, who wrote online, "Original minutes of the congregation board were in German and even into the 1960's the lighting for Friday night services, when Torah was read, stayed low and dark, European style."

## PITTSBURGH

*Beth David/Beth Abraham*
*346 Miller Street (near Foreside Place) | 15219*

There are two important Jewish markers on the front of this orangey brick building: a Jewish star made of recessed brick, and a small plaque that read "Bet David Congregation", above the windows that are above the main doors. It's curious that "Bet David" is rendered in Hebrew and "Congregation" is in English. A cornerstone to the right of the entrance reads "1905." The actual story of this congregation is convoluted: despite the Bet(h) David name, it only operated as such for a short while, due to mergers and name changes. (And why no one bothered to change the name is a quirk itself.) For a while they were known as ShaarayTefillah. Locally they were also called the "big Russian shul." They eventually moved in the 1940s to

Bartlett Street. There might be a time capsule incorporated into this Miller Street building.

*B'nai Israel*
*327 North Negley Avenue (at Rippey Street) | 15206*

Once a shul, then a school, now residential: the building still has a grand feel to it. This domed structure of stone and concrete has many lovely stained glass windows. The fantastic recessed entrance has a beautiful arch in front of it, with a Decalogue at the peak; but the main attraction is the beautiful mural above the main doors, which also features another Decalogue. This site was designed by Henry Hornbostel, Alexander Sharove and Philip Friedman. Further back in the campus, in the school building section (which was built later), there are interesting windows with abstract designs. When I saw the former synagogue in October 2019, vines of leaves had grown all over the main section, making the building quite pretty, if a bit haunted.

The older section of this lovely building dates to 1923, and was designated a historic landmark in 1979. However, it ceased serving as a shul in 1995, and the congregation merged with Beth Jacob of Kensington. Later it housed a charter school, and following 2021 it was renovated into a mixture of housing, a communal multi-use space, and part turned into an urban farm. They are listed in the American Synagogue Directory of 1960 with Rabbi Dr. Seymour J. Cohen and President Samuel Schreiber.

*Kether Torah (Kesser Torah)*
*2080 Webster Avenue (at Erin Street) | 15219*

This corner building of brown brick has a large Jewish star on the Erin Street side as well as the narrower Seal Street side (and both of these are made of wooden panels). Look at the building from a block away so that you can see the dome. The building itself is not remarkable aside from the dome and the two Jewish stars, but there are some windows with missing panels and wood boards. Look carefully for a partially scratched out cornerstone that reads "Erected 1920" (three other lines of text have been scratched out). Originally this was a Russian Jewish congregation, its members coming from Volinia. Thus it was also called Anshe Volinia. Rabbi Aaron Ashinsky served this group. Later as Kether Torah, they moved to Bartlett Street.

*Anshe Lebovitz*
*110 Erin Street (at Ishar Way) | 15219*

This modestly sized and styled building has a curious hourglass-like design above the main entrance. It seems to be a Jewish star that had parts of it removed. There appears to be a spackled-over cornerstone as well. From this former synagogue, you can catch a glimpse of the dome of the former Kether Torah, just a few blocks away. The congregation was founded in 1906. Lebe Kasden served as their rabbi from 1920–24.

*Adath Jeshurun*
*5641 East Liberty Blvd (at North St. Clair Street) | 15206*

This corner brick building has nice details, and is across the street from a grassy boulevard. Above the entrance,which features a trio of doors, is a small plaque that reads "Adath Jeshurun Congregation" in English. Above that is a small Jewish star and the shul name in faded Hebrew letters. On the North St. Clair side there is a doorway with a small sign above it that reads "Talmud Torah" in Hebrew. And on the Mathews Way side (an alleyway) there is a stained glass window with a Decalogue below it (rendered in Hebrew) and a decorative arch around it that features several small Jewish stars. Elsewhere there are a few more memorial plaques on the exterior, three in Hebrew (one for or from a Goldblum, another for or from a Gershon Davis) and another in English, "Presented by Mr. and Mrs. J. Goldblum". According to the Rauh Archives, Adath Jeshurun was founded in 1916 and chartered in 1918, and the building was completed in 1924. This was an Orthodox congregation, known as the "Margaretta Street Shul," because East Liberty previously was known as Margaretta Street. In 1978 they merged with another congregation, Cneseth Israel, and moved to Monroeville in 1996. They closed down there in 2002.

## HOMESTEAD

*Homestead Hebrew Congregation*
*335 East 10th Avenue (near McClure Street) | 15120*

This is a handsome reddish brick building that features seven narrow, round-topped windows that together resemble a menorah. When I visited this building in 2019 I did not see a pretty Decalogue-Jewish star-menorah plaque, which has since been uncovered by the church that now occupies the building. To the side of the main steps there is a cornerstone that reads "Organized 1894–5659/ Erected 1913–5673". This was the only congregation in the neighborhood, and was Orthodox. The original membership was largely of Hungarian and Lithuanian backgrounds. Their membership dropped after the 1950s, eventually they closed in 1992, and a church took over the building. Beth Shalom Congregation in Pittsburgh assumed the memorialization of Homestead, and took in the shul's Judaica. In the American Synagogue Directory of 1960 it is co-named Rodef Shalom; Rabbi Hyman Shapiro and President Jerome Schwartz helmed the congregation. Tammy Hepps, a historian-writer-genealogist, is perhaps the most important documentor of this congregation, and is related to an early member of the congregation.She created a vivid website called www.homesteadhebrews.com .

# Former Connecticut Synagogues

Connecticut has had its share of significant Jewish communities and still does. Many of the former synagogues in the Nutmeg State have been knocked down, but I was able to locate nine buildings that were previously home to synagogues. Most are now serving Christian congregations but one is being used as a community arts center. Bridgeport, Hartford, New Britain, Meriden, Norwalk and Stamford are all home to former synagogues.

## STAMFORD

*Agudath Sholom*
*25 Grove Street | 06901*

The key attraction at this former synagogue of brick and stone is the circular window above the main entrance. It features a Jewish star amidst twelve spokes and twelve smaller window panels. It's pretty and well maintained, and a fine homage to Judaism. Aside from that, look carefully to spot a Jewish star just above the main doors, in a glass window. In addition, on the sides of the building there are memorial windows that are kept nicely. This is a medium-sized synagogue but the church has added a large trapezoidal staircase and an additional school building. This synagogue was built in the 1930s to replace their earlier synagogue in Stamford which was destroyed in a fire, located on Greyrock Place. The congregation's history stretches back to 1889, when 22 founding members first organized as a congregation. According to the American Synagogue Directory of 1960 they were led by Rabbi Joseph H. Ehrenkranz and President Louis J. Kuriansky. In 1965, they moved to a new synagogue and they are still active there.

## NORWALK

*Beth Israel*
*31 Concord St (at South Main Street) | 06854*

This is one of the more unusual lost synagogues that I have come across, especially in the northeastern section of the US. A wood-paneled corner building with two domes and keyhole style windows all over, this building hearkens back to an earlier time. It is an eclectic mixture of New England house of worship tempered with Victorian touches and Rundbogenstil elements. No Judaica seems to remain on the exterior but it is still a fascinating building. It was built in 1906 for an Orthodox congregation, originally organized around 1865, but since 1972 a Baptist church has resided here. It is a lovely Moorish Revival style building, the only known (former) shul in the Nutmeg State displaying Moorish onion domes. In addition it is remarkable for being a wood-frame one-time synagogue building and is on the National Register of Historic Places.The congregation became a Chabad group and moved to another location.

## BRIDGEPORT

*Ahavath Achim*
*724 Hancock Street (near State Street) | 06605*

The former Ahavath Achim resembles many a New England church, but there are Judaic reminders of its previous incarnation. Look carefully and see the Decalogue with Hebrew words (and peeling paint) in the pediment above the entrance. Above the main door is this English inscription, in an arc: "This is the gate of the Lord/ The righteous shall enter into it." Look up while at the door, to see another Jewish star on the ceiling. On one side of the building there are pretty stained glass windows, one with a handsome lion, Jewish star, and floral patterns. Another window also has the florals, a Jewish star and a pretty nature scene. Most of the building is of reddish brick but the front is wooden. Their first rabbi, who arrived in 1920, was Solomon Schulson. They moved out of this building in the late 1950s and have been located in Fairfield since then.

*B'nai Israel*
*1100 Park Avenue (near Laurel Avenue) | 06604*

This former synagogue has a cute look to it, and there is a remaining Decalogue near the roofline with Roman numerals. There is a little "1910" medallion above the main entrance. It was commonly known as the Park Avenue Temple, and they moved out of this building in the late 1950s. But the actual roots of the congregation go back to the 1850s, with German Jewish immigrant families.

*Rodeph Sholom/ Bikur Cholim*
*1541 Iranistan Avenue (at Maplewood Avenue) | 06604*

What appears to be a house with white clapboard siding and an add-on ramp is actually a brick building with several stained glass memorial windows. This was once the home of Bikur Cholim and is now a church. There is a small, plain Decalogue above the main doors.

Built around 1894 for a Congregational church, this building housed two different Jewish congregations from 1929 to 1989. The building is an example of the Shingle Style of architecture, and was listed on the National Register of Historic Places in 1995.

The first shul here was Congregation Rodeph Sholom, which used the building from 1923 until 1949 when they moved to Capitol Avenue, and then came Congregation Bikur Cholim which used the building until the congregation moved in 1989.

## MERIDEN

*B'nai Abraham*
*127 East Main Street | 06450*

This expansive former synagogue with manicured lawns still retains Jewish stars in several places: above the main entrance and on two sets of hand railings. There are other pretty details present on this brick edifice, such as a Decalogue with Hebrew words just above the main door, but it's kind of a winding, unusually shaped structure overall. This building dates to 1952; prior to this the congregation was located on Cedar Street. According to Google Maps, as of July 2018 you could still see the name of the synagogue on the main section of the building (Temple B'nai Abraham) in metal letters, as well as a pretty menorah sculpture attached to the downhill segment of the building. In the American Synagogue Directory of 1960 we learn that their rabbi was Albert N. Troy. B'nai Abraham merged with Congregation Adath Israel in 2019.

## NEW BRITAIN

*Temple B'nai Israel*
*265 West Main Street (at Russell Street) | 06052*

This big corner building, a stately neo-classical construction set back on raised lawns, is an impressive former synagogue resembling other lost synagogues in Detroit, Chicago, Syracuse and elsewhere. It still says "Temple B'nai Israel" over the main entrance of four thick columns and three doorways. It looks a bit out of place amongst the private homes surrounding it. The light-colored brick and details are all in very good shape, although the steps in the front need upkeep. Above the door on Russell Street it still says "Temple B'nai Israel." The church here now used to have a banner hanging, but took it down and only has a very modest sign on the side. It was built in 1929 as a Masonic hall, and became the shul in 1940 (then known as Aheyu B'nai Israel). The synagogue closed mid-year in 2007.

## HARTFORD

*Congregation Temple Beth Israel*
*25 Charter Oak Avenue (near Main Street) | 06106*

This building is grand, and important in the history of Jewish Connecticut, as it was the "first building in the state built as a synagogue," according to the plaque by the front doors. It is a beautiful red brick building, in an eclectic style. The two domes and the dormer between them are above a set of five pretty windows. It is now used as a cultural arts center with multiple uses.

The side near Main Street has a delightful garden. According to the Jewish Heritage Center at New England Historic Genealogical Society, which has the archival collection for the congregation, Beth Israel was founded in 1843 and started out as Orthodox. Later it became Reform. This building was their home from the mid 1870s through 1935. Now the congregation is in another location.

*Beth Hamedrash Hagadol*
*370 Garden Street | 06112*

Located in the middle of a block, the only real indicator of this building now serving as a church is a free-standing sign. Otherwise the details are all Judaic in nature. This is a nicely designed brick building in an open-Torah style, three parts, with lancet windows and three small Jewish stars (two between doorway arches, one in the middle of the large rose window). In the back of the building there is another Jewish star in the middle of a rose window. According to the American Synagogue Directory of 1960 their rabbi was Irving Singer and their president was Ely Waxman. The architects of this building were Julius Berenson and Jacob Moses. The shul had merged with another, Shaarey Torah, in the East Side. They resided here from the early 1920s through 1962, when they merged with another congregation and moved to West Hartford.

# Former Chicago Synagogues

The greater Chicago area has long been home to a large Jewish community, comprising various subgroups. A large city that has posh neighborhoods, middle class areas and heavily crime-ridden districts, the Jewish community has left its mark throughout much of the city. In fact, for many years Chicago was considered to have the third largest Jewish population among the world's cities. Thus there are many extant former synagogues, while others were demolished.

I was able to view more than seventy synagogues and could have located more, according to my research. The synagogue, school and Jewish institutional buildings that I found (including a few that are active) can be seen throughout a great swath of Chicago. I spent two jam-packed days driving around and photographing them. However, I am not including discussion here of most that seemed not to have any visible Judaica on the exterior.

It was important for me to revisit Chicago and see these former synagogues. I visited with my family in August 2010, and we went to the typical tourist attractions and museums. During that trip I attended a weekday morning service at the Chicago Loop Synagogue in the downtown area, with its beautiful stained glass windows. In passing I had noticed one former synagogue while we rode by on a city bus. But the purpose of my trip then had been family fun, not documenting lost synagogues.

I had the chance to take a quick trip to Chicago in November 2023, snagging inexpensive airplane tickets. This trip was almost completely devoted to viewing former synagogues, and I was particularly interested in seeing how they are arranged within the various neighborhoods of Chicago. Some of the areas are in very good condition, a few were rough at the edges, and a few are quite rundown.

Something eerie happened to me in Chicago that has not happened anywhere else within the US. I stopped my car on the 1300 block of South

Keeler Avenue. I sat in the car and snapped a few photographs of a former synagogue, and then heard the sound of one of the car handles being grabbed and rattled. Fortunately all the car doors were locked, but I shouted a few curse words and accelerated away swiftly. I looked in the rear view mirror and took note of the man who had tried to open the car door.

Unnerved and mildly angered, I took it in stride. Nothing happened to me, and overall I enjoyed my brief visit to Chicago. I conducted meaningful research, saw several gorgeous former synagogues as well as those more modest, and was pleased to have made this my last major destination for research.

I had one other slightly annoying experience, which I have dealt with previously: while photographing a former Jewish building that is now used as a school, I was confronted by a woman who demanded to know why I was taking pictures "or are you just randomly taking photographs?" I turned to her and said coolly "I'm photographing this because it used to be a Jewish community building. I'm doing research." She seemed a bit mollified by my explanation.

The former synagogues of Chicago range in size from very modest to very large. Most were from the first half of the 1900s, a few much later. Many are still in very good shape, with prominent Judaica still remaining on the exteriors. Others were in poor condition. A few featured official historic site plaques, informing passersby that these buildings had originally been built and used as synagogues, even if they now house churches, private residences and such.

A large percentage are now used as churches, but others are private homes, community centers, schools. The building usages are similar to those seen in other major American cities such as New York, Newark, Philadelphia, Detroit. I was pleased to see that many retain Judaica on the outside sections, but I was unable to get inside any of the buildings, mostly because I was there on a Tuesday and a Wednesday. Many even had gates up but I was able to look inside the lobbies of a few.

There were a large handful that are still greatly impressive buildings, and I gushed over them. These tend to be in very good shape, with intricate details and features. Another aspect I noticed is that the majority of these Chicago lost shuls have generic names, such as B'nai Zion, Temple Beth El, Agudas Achim, Sinai Temple. There are not as many (remaining?) synagogues with foreign place-names, which is more common in New York City. Examples of these include the Austrian Galician Shul and First

Roumanian Congregation. The Lawndale neighborhood has several, such as Anshe Pavalatch, Ohel Jacob Am Kovno, Anshe Mozir, Anshe Odessa, and others. In addition I was able to see more than one former home for a few congregations.

The two sources I used initially for research on names and locations of former synagogues in Chicago were the American Jewish Yearbook, which I consulted for many other states, cities, and towns; and the Chicago Bike Adventures website. Briefly I considered renting a bike, but I am glad that I rented a car because the neighborhoods cover a great amount of space.

I did not visit every city in the United States, but aside from NYC, Chicago seems to me to have the largest number of former synagogues and related institutions still standing. Similar to NYC, Chicago's lost shuls are found in several neighborhoods throughout the city: among them are Rogers Park in the north, Albany Park and Budlong Woods not too far from there, Logan Square and Wicker Park a bit south. A much larger concentration is found further south from there, especially in North Lawndale and Lawndale, Douglass Park and Homan Square. Going further southeast there are some in the Bronzeville and Fuller Park region and South Shore.

As with parts of Brooklyn, the Bronx, Manhattan and even Detroit and Philadelphia, I wondered how sections of Chicago had so many synagogues close together. Why did members of the Jewish community think that so many shuls, in dense concentration, could survive? And sadly, these many buildings are now former, not active synagogues. It would be hard to sustain so many, especially bigger buildings, even in a heavily Jewish neighborhood.

By tallying up how many former synagogues there are by zip code, we can see which areas had the greatest historic concentration of these buildings. By far the most remaining lost synagogues and similar buildings can be found within 60623, where I located 21 such sites. Many of these sites are large, and some are what I would consider extra large. The Jewish community must have been large, devoted, and ambitious to build so many Jewish sites here, at least for a certain period of time.

Robert Packer, an author and tireless researcher on Chicago's Jewish community over the years, has done an impressive job documenting former and current congregations.

*Congregation Beth Israel Anshe Yanova*
*1328 West Morse Avenue | 60626*

For some years this charming, midblock former synagogue has been a commercial establishment. It has a pretty roofline and other aspects, but the Judaica is gone. House of Israel-Men of Yanova, was an Orthodox shul located earlier at 3905 West 14th Street in the old North Lawndale neighborhood. Founded in the 1930s, this congregation had members who came from the city of Yanova in Lithuania. The shul's Board elected to move to the Rogers Park neighborhood in 1955. In the 1970s, Beth Israel Anshe Yanova moved to suburban Skokie. Among their rabbis were Melvyn Rush and Yehuda D. Goldman. The American Synagogue Directory of 1960 lists Rabbi Bernard D. Perlow and President Alex O. Weingart as their leaders.

*Temple Mizpah*
*1615 West Morse Avenue (near North Ashland Avenue) | 60626*

This medium-large former synagogue has an interesting motif of windows and cast-stone decorations that resemble Decalogues. These stylistic elements are the main clue to its Jewish past. At one point the temple merged and became Temple Judea Mizpah. Originally founded in 1919, Temple Mizpah built a modern community center with a Hebrew school and sanctuary that was designed in 1922 by the Chicago architectural firm of Spitzer and Popkin. Rabbi Jacob Singer, Rabbi Joseph Buchler and Rabbi Martin Silverman were among their spiritual leaders.

*B'nai Zion*
*1447 West Pratt Boulevard (by North Greenview Avenue) | 60626*

It still reads "B'nai Zion Synagogue" at this handsome building, and there is a Decalogue with Hebrew words still visible near the roofline. The main entrance section of this former synagogue is full of delicate details, including two menorahs and an eternal flame design. An interesting touch can be found just above a door at one end of the building, which has two fantastic animals facing each other. Founded in 1919, Congregation B'nai Zion began worshipping in a repurposed church (St. Paul's By The Lake), and by 1928 erected its Moorish Byzantine style sanctuary, designed by Chicago architect Edward Perry Steinberg. In 1949 they added the Wolberg Community Center. Their long-serving spiritual leaders included Rabbi A. L.

Lassen, followed by Rabbi Henry Fisher, Rabbi Morris Fishman and Rabbi David Lincoln. One of their presidents was Abraham Finkelstein. Due to changing demographics, and a declining and aging membership,they sold their campus to Lake Shore School in 2002. B'nai Zion then merged with North Park Shaare Tikvah. Among their communal activities was a USY chapter for the children.

*Congregation Kesser Maariv*
*6418 North Greenview Avenue | 60626*

Here is one of the most unusual reuses for a former synagogue; it is now a museum, The Leather Archives and Museum. The congregation is still active in nearby Skokie, and its full name is now Beth Hamedrash Hagadol Kesser Maariv, but usually just Kesser Maariv. Their roots go back to 1867, and they tout themselves as the "oldest Orthodox congregation in the Midwest." They moved and experienced mergers a few times. The building at this location was built in the 1950s; earlier they worshipped in this spot, but in an old house. In 1989 and 1990, the shul building was the victim of violent incidents (gang related) and they vacated at the end of 1990. For a few years they worshiped in Rabbi Lazovsky's home, then moved to Skokie in 1994.

*B'nai Jacob Congregation*
*6200 North Artesian Avenue (at West Granville Avenue) | 60659*

The front of this stately building still reads B'nai Jacob Congregation, and there are still two Decalogues with Hebrew letters above the name. The West Granville side has pretty stained glass memorial windows as well. We read in the American Synagogue Directory of 1960 that they were led by Rabbi Joseph A. Gorfinkel and President Melvin White. But in the summer of 1962 there was news coverage in The Sentinel (Voice of Chicago Jewry) of Dr. Louis Sacks assuming the pulpit. The shul was built in 1952. Dale Lind was the cantor in the 1950s and 1960s. They left this site in the late 1990s. Their Hebrew school was located across the street diagonally at 2447 West Granville Avenue; both these buildings are two different churches.The exterior of the West Granville building had a menorah design up through 2019, according to Google Maps, but in recent years the church there covered it up with a banner.

*Congregation Lev Someach*
*5555 North Bernard Street (at West Bryn Mawr Avenue) | 60659*

This is a modest post WW2 corner building with a cornerstone that reads 1955/5715, and that is the primary remainder of its Jewish past. Now it is used as an office building for Northeastern Illinois University. According to Robb Packer on Facebook, the shul was here from 1955–1980 but had other, earlier locations including one in the North Lawndale area. Members of the Twersky family have been rabbis here (they come from a Hasidic dynasty) and Arnold F. Block was a president.

*Kehilath Jeshurun Synagogue*
*3707 West Ainslie Street (at North Lawndale Avenue) | 60625*

This building sports pretty mottled brick and a few modified Jewish stars still remain, along with stained glass memorial windows. "Erected 1940" is etched in a stone by the main doors.

Founded as the Hebrew Institute of Albany Park and built in 1940, it became the permanent home of Kehilat Jeshuren Synagogue a few years later. Rabbi Nathan was a long-serving spiritual leader, but the American Synagogue Directory of 1960 lists Rabbi Nathan Levinson and President Robert Burnstein. Some of the stained glass windows designed by artist David Bekker were saved, donated and restored by former Judge Jerry Orbach for another Jewish site. In the 1970s the building was sold to Cross and Crown Church.

*Temple Beth Israel*
*4850 North Bernard Street (at West Ainslie Street) | 60625*

There are a few quite impressive elements remaining on this building from its days as a synagogue. Above the entrance there are two Lions of Judah that face each other, with a plain decalogue in the middle. But the Hebrew above this is notable: it is the three word quote *V'Ahavta Lereiacha Kamocha*, usually translated to English as "You shall love your fellow man as yourself." The extension section of the building has three partial Jewish stars which are obscured by modern windows. The columns near the main entrance are of a Corinthian style.

This was a Reform congregation, founded in 1917, often meeting at community halls on Lawrence Avenue and Kedzie Avenue. In 1923 they dedicated the cornerstone to their new Temple, later building a community center and Hebrew school in 1927. Their long-serving spiritual leaders were Rabbi S. Felix Mendelsohn and Rabbi Ernst M. Lorge. One of their shul presidents was Leonard Fuchs. In the early 1960s they established a "satellite" site in suburban Skokie, and moved there fully in 1981.

*Beth Jacob*
*4920 North Kimball Avenue | 60625*

This two-building complex is midblock and while it doesn't have a special flare, there are a few peculiar clues to its Jewish past. Look at the railings at the steps of the smaller building, and you will see ten partial Jewish stars. Each star has had the top and bottom sections removed, but they are still quite obviously Jewish stars that have been modified. According to Robb Packer on the Synagogues of Chicago Facebook page, the actual date of founding is unclear but it preceded the building of the Beth Jacob Youth Center in 1956 by founding spiritual leader and principal Rabbi Haskell Lehrfield. Later the Hebrew School building was sold for use as the Henry Hart JCC. Still later Beth Jacob sold their campus to a Korean-American Church. The American Synagogue Directory of 1960 states that their president was Ben Stiebel.

*B'nai David Budlong Conservative Jewish Center*
*2626 West Foster Avenue | 60625*

Designed in 1958 by the Chicago architectural team of Housner and Macsai, this congregation dates back further to 1903. Later B'nai David merged with Shaare Zedek and sold their building to a church. According to the American Synagogue Directory of 1960 they were helmed by Rabbi Murry J. Peiman and President Harry Kirman.

*Agudas Achim*
*5029 North Kenmore Avenue | 60640*

This is a gorgeous, regal building that bucks the trend of synagogues becoming churches; no, this structure was renovated into stylish apartments. A sign in English, above the main entrance, still reads Agudath Achim North Shore Congregation, spelled out in an interesting font. Above the uppermost window you still see a Jewish star and a Decalogue. The building has the appearance of a theater, with nice flourishes. Now this is a residential building dubbed "The Synagogue," and it has a parking lot. According to "Synagogues of Chicago," the congregation was founded in 1905 and commissioned this building, designed by the architectural firm Dubin and Eisenberg. The congregation worshiped here through 2008, and they were experiencing legal problems by then. It sat abandoned and graffitied for a few years before the major renovation. In fact, there are at least a dozen articles on the internet about the building and its rebirth.The congregation modified its name a few times and at least one other group merged into them, North Shore Sons of Israel. The original founders of Agudas Achim were Hungarian Jews.The American Synagogue Directory of 1960 lists their rabbi as Sidney B. Risback and their president Joseph J. Klein.

*Congregation Anshe Emes*
*627 West Patterson Avenue | 60613*

Located on a block of stylish apartment buildings, this former synagogue still features the name "Anshe Emes" in English, over the main entrance. This Conservative congregation goes back to 1873 and had a few different earlier homes. In fact, this location was only used from 1922 to 1929; they then moved elsewhere in the city and are still active, as Anshe Emet. The Patterson location was designed by Jacob Aroner. But Congregation Anshe Mizrach then moved into the site. Now this building is an apartment building.

*Temple Emanuel*
*701 West Buckingham Place | 60657*

It still says Temple Emanuel on this building, and there are a few other nice touches remaining from the synagogue days. The block it's located on is a pleasant collection of small apartment buildings and private homes. Later called Emanuel Congregation, it was founded in 1880 and became Reform in 1889. After several temporary moves, the congregation built their first permanent sanctuary in 1907, then rebuilt after a horrific fire in 1916. In 1955 Temple Emanuel sold their site to a Japanese Church Group, which was later sold to a developer to become the first Chicago temple to be converted to condos (known as Buckingham Pews). The congregation has been at North Sheridan Road for decades now.

*Beth-El Center*
*3238 West Palmer Street (at North Sawyer Avenue) | 60647*

This former synagogue has an intriguing sign near the roofline: the English words Knowledge, Justice and Truth are interspersed with the Hebrew words *Da'at, Avodah* and *Emet*. (These are direct translations.) Beth-El Center and two Jewish stars are above the main entrance, and according to Google Maps, up until late 2018 a church had covered up the synagogue's name with a banner, but now that is easy to read.This brick building is a basic boxy style but with several nice decorative touches, in addition to the tenets listed up above. Now it is not used as a house of worship, but as apartments. Founded in 1871, they had a few other homes prior to this site. The West Palmer home dates to 1923 and was designed by Edward Perry Steinberg. Later in the 1950s they sold their campus to the Chicago Boys Club (Boys and Girls Club of Chicago).

*B'nai David-Ohave Zedek*
*1910 North Humboldt Boulevard (near West Cortland St) | 60647*

Located on a pretty boulevard with grassy malls, this former synagogue still has a presence. The building is a neoclassical treat, and the name of the congregation is easily read in English, located just below the pediment. Two Jewish stars are just below the name, each on an Ionic pilaster.There is also a Decalogue with Hebrew writing above the main entrance. The church there now is keeping the building in good shape. Founded in 1903 through the merger of B'nai David (1903) and Ohave Zedek (1889), this synagogue was designed by Chicago architect David Saul Klafter in 1919. It was familiarly known as the Humboldt Boulevard Temple. Later it merged with the Budlong Conservative Center (1959) and moved to another building, a mid-century styled site.

*North West Hebrew Congregation*
*1847 North Kildare Avenue | 60639*

The former North West Hebrew Congregation has one remaining symbol of its Judaic past, a Jewish star near the roofline, in the middle of the building. There are other original details present in this brick building but they are more abstract, not specifically Jewish.

*Congregation Zemach Zedek*
*1459 North Talman Avenue (at West LeMoyne Street) | 60622*

This former synagogue looks different than most of the others surveyed here. While many of the Chicago lost shuls have a neoclassical style or are boxy buildings that were made more elaborate with decorative touches, the former Zemach Zedek is in another category, particularly because it was built as a church in 1892. One way in which it is similar to several others is that its name is still visible: in a sign above the main entrance you can read in Hebrew "Cong. Tzemach Tzedek V'Hevrat Tehillim." The sign also has two Jewish stars. Other parts of the building were bricked up or painted over, and the LeMoyne Street side is worn down, but seen from the front, this is still a proud, attractive house of worship. The shul resided here from the 1920s through 1960s.

*Austro-Galician Shul*
*1357 North California Avenue (at West Hirsch Street) | 60622*

The former Austro-Galician Congregation is one of the Chicago former synagogues that has "ghosting" Hebrew words, faint Hebrew that has greatly faded and is difficult to read. (You can see this on lost synagogues in New York City and elsewhere, as well.) You can also find spots where Jewish stars seem to have been removed, such as above the main doors at the front entrance. This is a shame and it's not clear if this was done by the church or even by the Jewish congregation before it vacated. Aside from this it is a well-kept brick building on a corner. However, on the West Hirsch side of the building you can see at least a dozen stained glass windows that still retain Jewish stars within their designs. The congregation goes back to the 1890s, and this building dates to the early 1910s. They merged and moved with another congregation in the 1950s.The world famous Metropolitan Opera star singer Richard Tucker had a stint as a cantor here during the High Holy Days one year. One of their leaders was Rabbi Moses Eichenstein.

*Atereth Zion Community Synagogue*
*1132 North Spaulding Avenue | 60651*

If this former synagogue did not have a few Jewish stars and its name spelled out in Hebrew, nor have a church sign, you might think it was actually a theater, based on the decorative touches on the front of the building.

It still has two Jewish star medallions, over two of the three main doors. (This building, like some other Chicago Jewish sites, has three doors and three main windows.) The name Atereth Zion is written in Hebrew above the upper level windows. At the very top of the building is a stand-alone medallion with a Jewish star; it looks like a necklace charm. Over the past several years the church sign has changed a few times, according to Google Maps photos.This was an Orthodox congregation, familiarly known as the Spaulding Avenue Shul. Their long-time spiritual leader was Rabbi Nathan H. Gordon and their cantor was Anchell Friedman. One shul president was Harry P. Steinberg. Atereth Zion was founded in the 1920s and erected this iconic synagogue in 1928. It was the largest synagogue on the Westside of Humboldt Park, closing in 1965.

*Congregation B'nai Israel of Austin & Hebrew School*
*5433 West Jackson Boulevard | 60644*

In the middle of a quiet residential block, this former shul-and-school campus remains as a stately and well-kept reminder of a Jewish past. The smaller, simpler school building at 5435 has at least two visible Jewish stars at the second floor, and two menorah designs near each side of the main entrance. The larger, fancier synagogue building at 5433 shows two Jewish stars on the second level, and in an arch above the middle pair of second floor windows it reads in Hebrew "Congregation B'nai Israel." This is not easy to read; one needs to be at the right angle to see this. According to Google Maps, in 2008 there was a cross attached to the building but that has since been removed. Overall this building looks quite good, with just a few pieces of wear and tear visible from the outside. Founded in the 1920s, B'nai Israel built its classically designed synagogue in 1927, designed by the noted Chicago architectural team of Lechinko and Esser. They built their community center in 1949. Their spiritual leaders were Rabbi A.E. Abramowitz, Rabbi Louis Lehrfield and Rabbi Shlomoh Z. Fineberg. One of their synagogue presidents was George Edelstein. According to Chicago-Ancestors, B'nai Israel of Austin sold their campus in 1970 and repurposed a storefront in the West Ridge community (this information has not been independently verified). Today this former synagogue is occupied by The Bethel Apostolic Church.

*B'nai Sholom of Garfield Park*
*4416 West Gladys Avenue | 60624*

At least three different churches have resided in this building that once was home to a synagogue. There is one remaining Jewish star near the peaked roof, and it seems to have rusted and lost a few pieces. Overall this is a small, modest lost synagogue. They were also located at 4335 W. Harrison Street, which was demolished). Their long-time spiritual leader was Rabbi Benjamin Baim, but the American Synagogue Directory of 1960 lists Rabbi Nathan I. Weiss and President Aaron Becker.

*Congregation Anshe Sholom*
*3808 West Polk Street/754 South Independence Boulevard | 60624*

The former Anshe Sholom is one of the Chicago former synagogues that displays trios of features. In this case, there are three large stained glass windows on the second story (each with a Jewish star and other decoration), and below that are three doors. The pediment at the top features a Decalogue with Hebrew, and what appear to be waves or clouds, for accent. The cornerstone at Polk-South Independence features the Hebrew name "Bet Haknesset Anshe Sholom" and the dates, but the only English word that is legible is "Congregation." The sole major feature from the church that resides here now is the sign with the name, above the main entrance doors. According to the American Synagogue Directory of 1960 they were led by Rabbi Benzion C. Kaganoff and President I.M. Friedman. This neoclassical synagogue was designed by the architectural firm Alexander Levy & Associates

*Congregation Atereth Israel Anshe Ticktin*
*1230 South Millard Avenue | 60623*

In the middle of a residential block of one and two family homes, stands this attractive, medium-sized former synagogue. Although some parts have been bricked in or over, much of the Judaica does remain visible. Among these details are the name "Congregation Atereth Israel Anshe Ticktin" in English, in an arch, and a smaller version in Hebrew, just above the doorway. Over the Hebrew is an elaborate design with a Jewish star in the center. There are other original patterns and abstract elements that give it a nice appearance. The church did make a simple cross out of glass, and added in a free standing sign. This is one of the old former shuls from which retired judge Jerry Orbach has saved stained glass windows. According to the Facebook page Synagogues of Chicago, they merged with Mikro Kodesh Lida and Pinsk, and had a building at 2832 West Foster. (Note that Tiktin is a Yiddishized version of the city Tykocin.)

*Kehilath Jacob*
*3757 West Douglas Boulevard (at South Hamlin Avenue) | 60623*

Look up to see "Khelath-Jacob" in English and three Jewish stars on the front of this classical Revival style building, located on a corner. There are well-kept pilasters and other trim details on this building, and the only real clue of its contemporary use are two discrete signs for the church. The architect was Abraham L Himmelblau and it was built in 1915–16. In 1956 the building was sold and they merged and moved to a new synagogue at 3701 West Devon, forming Congregation Kehilath Jacob-Beth Samuel.

*First Roumanian Congregation*
*3622 West Douglas Boulevard (at South Millard Avenue) | 60623*

With stained glass Jewish stars on the Boulevard side and the Avenue side, this corner building still looks quite like a synagogue. The front of this building is so nicely balanced: three doors, three large sets of windows (each with two sets of three smaller windows), and a single Decalogue (with Hebrew words) set within a pattern that looks woven. The church set up one demure sign and a few banners. Overall it seems to be in very good condition. The congregation was founded in the late 1890s, as First Roumanian Shaare Shamayim (Gates of Heaven). This building was designed by Joseph W. Cohen & Co. and built in the mid-1920s. Rabbi Harris Goldstein was their longtime spiritual leader. In the 1950s, First Roumanian sold their building to Stone Temple Baptist Church where Dr. Martin Luther King Jr. preached to this assembly.

*Synagogue & Marks Nathan Jewish Orphan Home*
*1564 South Albany Avenue | 60623*

This is one of the larger former Jewish institutions in Chicago; it spans a full block. Most of it is the former Orphan Home. For several years a sign in all capital letters that says "Marks Nathan Jewish Orphan Home" was covered by another sign that read "Sacred Heart Home," but according to Google Maps, by 2018 that was removed and the original sign was again visible. This brick building is three stories high, and the synagogue at the 16th Street edge is the same height. The sole Judaic element there is the Jewish star inside the portico above the original main entrance. Marks Nathan Jewish Orphan Home was also known as Marks Nathan Hall. Founded in 1903 on the NorthWest side, this building was erected in 1911.

*Anshe Pavalatch*
*1539 South Christiana Avenue | 60623*

A small former synagogue that has seen much better days, this mid-block building seems to have been altered considerably over time. It has one identifier from the synagogue's time, a cast stone sign above the entrance in Hebrew that reads "Congregation Anshe Pavalitch" and below it "Nusach Sfard." A few letters have faded. The stone arch below this seems to have ghosted Hebrew letters, letters that for the most part have been faded or scraped off. Yet another English spelling for the place-name is Pavolitch. A familial name for the shul was the Turner Avenue Shul because that was the street name before it was Christiana. There is a group called the United Pavolitcher Society, a landsmanschaft/benevolent society.

*Ohel Jacob Anshe Kovno*
*1448 South Homan Avenue (at West 15th Street) | 60623*

The former Anshe Kovno, like many other former shuls in Chicago, is located on a corner. It has a Decalogue at the peak of the roof, with Hebrew writing and two Jewish stars still visible. It has a vaguely neo-classical look to it, with some windows bricked in, as at other former area shuls. But it has one particularly remarkable feature, a Juliet balcony of cast stone that has another Jewish star. This is quite pretty, and fortunately it has held up over time. An alternate spelling for this Lithuanian town is Kaunas. The building dates to the early 1920s and it had a previous location on West Peoria Street and 14th Place.

*Anshe Lubovitch*
*3535 West 15th Street (at South Drake Avenue) | 60623*

This former synagogue, a brick structure on a corner, has much of its front bricked over, which is a shame. There are a few pleasant touches, including a series of Decalogue designs near the roofline (without writing or numbers) and one noticeable Jewish star. But mostly it looks woebegone, and the steps are crumbling. Across the street is another former synagogue and that one has its former main entrance completely bricked up (Beth Jacob Anshe Kroz). Many years ago this must have been a vibrant Jewish block. It was the first Chabad synagogue in Chicago, established in 1875.

*Beth Jacob Anshe Kroz*
*3540 West 15th Street (at South Drake Avenue) | 60623*

Just across from the former Anshe Lubovitch is this former synagogue, a reddish-brown brick building that appears to have once been rather commanding. But now, with its Judaica stripped and other parts bricked up, it has a muted appearance. Two modest doorways and a few windows are the only sign of life here. According to a post on the Forgotten Chicago Discussion Group, the building was designed by Abraham Himelblau and built 1919–20. It was impressive, with two domes and two lion statues. The congregation moved out in the mid-1950s and merged with Beth Sholom Ahavas Achim on West Douglass Boulevard. In 2011 a big fire devastated the building but the church rebuilt parts of it.

*Congregation Anshe Odessa*
*1626 South Lawndale Avenue | 60623*

There is little obvious Judaica remaining at this former shul, a brick building with a bit of scalloping present, except for two visible Jewish stars at the first floor and two close to the roofline, in bricked up windows. Most of the previous entrance was bricked over. The building was designed by Clarence P. Leavitt and built in 1923, according to photographer Brule Laker. It closed in 1952. Previous to this location it was on Hastings Street.

*Congregation Anshe Motele*
*3737 West 18th Street (at South Ridgeway Avenue) | 60623*

Although essentially a simple box shape, the former Anshe Motele is an attractive corner building of dark brown brick and concrete. The roofline has an unusual, interesting design which brings to mind an embroidery pattern. Several Jewish stars can still be seen in windows throughout the building, and most important, the main entrance reads "Cong. Anshe Motele" in English, and in Hebrew "Cong. Ezrat Yisrael Anshe Motele" along with decorative medallions. The church there now added only two small signs. This Orthodox congregation lives on, now located at N. California Avenue, but it was founded in 1903, according to JGSI, Jewish Genealogical Society of Illinois. (Motel was in Russia, now Belarus.) It was also referred to as the Carpenters Shul.

*Isaiah Temple*
*4505 South Vincennes Avenue (at East 45th St) | 60653*

This corner building may have a red-and-white neon sign at the very edge that reads "Ebenezer Baptist Church" and has another narrow sign, but most of this building still resembles the synagogue it was built as, Isaiah Temple. In fact that name, in English, is easy to see over the main doors. The front and the 45th Street side have a handful of pretty half-circle floral design windows. The brickwork is in good shape, and there are other nice neo-classical details here. The complex is composed of two buildings of matching brick. The smaller building has a nice abstract window, running almost its full height, that seems to be of a later design. (I have seen that style on other lost synagogues in New York City, for example.) It was a Reform synagogue, designed by Dankmar Adler as his last commission. It was dedicated in 1899 (cornerstone laid in 1898). In 1924 Isaiah merged with B'nai Sholom Temple Israel to form Isaiah Israel and in 1971 it merged with KAM, Kehilath Anshe Ma'arav, one of the oldest congregations with several well-known members.

*Sinai Temple*
*4600 South MLKing Jr. Boulevard (at East 46th Street) | 60653*

On a wide, tree lined boulevard, this weighty former synagogue is the essence of neo-classical design. The familiar quote is rendered here as "Mine

House Shall Be/ A House Of Prayer For All Nations," as an engraved "banner" across the front entrance. The church there now placed its name sign underneath, and added a lawn sign around 2017 (as seen on Google Maps) but for the most part it still has the look of the synagogue. The East 46th Street side of the building is also very impressive but doesn't have Judaic markers. Little clues reveal the history of the main building, such as a small sign on the 46th Street side in the middle of a pediment that reads "5670." The building was designed by Alfred Samuel Alschuler in 1912 and the building now houses a church. The congregation lives on at a different location, at West Delaware Place.

*Beth Hamedrash Hagadol*
*5129 South Indiana Avenue (near East 51st Street) | 60615*

There might not be another former synagogue in Chicago that has as many visible Jewish stars as the former Beth Hamedrash Hagadol. Although the majority of them are subtle, worked into decorative patterns, once you notice them they are impressive. They run up and down much of the front of the building, in four lines. There are a few other Jewish stars elsewhere, a Decalogue with Hebrew lettering, and the congregation's name in English, on a plaque. This medium-sized building may not be as elaborate as some other Chicago sites surveyed here, but those Jewish stars are special. According to Carey Wintergreen on the Facebook page Bronzeville Alliance, the architect for the building was Alexander L. Levy and it was built in 1916. They stayed here until 1933, and moved to Greenwood Avenue (which they also left).

*Temple B'nai Sholom*
*5310 South Michigan Avenue (at East 53rd Street) | 60615*

Anchoring a corner, this grand brick former shul has some classical touches to it, such as the four Ionic pilasters. There is a Jewish star at the peak of the roof, and one other right above the central of three doors. There are several well-kept stained glass windows throughout the building, Curiously, there are two cornerstones at the 53rd Street end, one that reads "1937" and the lower that reads "1913." The one from 1937 is from the church, the earlier one from the synagogue. This classic temple was designed by renowned Chicago architect Alfred S. Alschuler in 1913. B'nai Sholom (1852) merged with Temple Israel (1898) at 44th Street and St. Lawrence Avenue to become B'nai Sholom Temple Israel. Later they merged with Isaiah Temple in 1924 to form Isaiah Israel at Hyde Park Boulevard and Greenwood Avenue. (This lineage is a bit tangled, and leaves a few neo-classical former synagogues in its wake!)

*Hebrew School, Anshe Dorum*
*125 East 59th Street (at South Michigan Avenue) | 60637*

This solid-looking building has some pretty reminders of its Jewish past as a religious school: the five menorahs of cast stone embedded on the second floor, a Decalogue near the roofline. The brickwork has held up nicely but many of the windows need fixing. The vaguely Gothic entrance has an obvious cross, which is more jarring than the church's sign. It was built in 1915.

*Congregation B'nai Bezalel*
*6034 South Champlain Avenue | 60637*

Mostly faced with sandy colored brick, the front of this former synagogue is made somewhat dramatic because of the trio of lengthy windows in the middle. Over time, the name of the congregation was sometimes visible, sometimes covered by a sign for a church, but more recently it has been exposed again. Apparently B'nai Bezalel was the first shul in the Woodlawn area, built in the early 1920s for $250,000. The sanctuary could seat 1,500. Two other congregations merged with this group: Beth Jacob in 1927 and Anshe Misrach in 1928.

They moved out in the 1940s to another space. But now it has become a home and a creative arts space, renovated by a family. Several news articles, including one from Preserving Chicago, have documented this.

*Congregation Anshe Emeth*
*1122 West 61st Street | 60621*

This is a medium-sized brick building and a bit disheveled. There is nothing left of the Judaic past here on the West 61st Street side, but on the South May Street side the doorway arch still reads "Cong. Anshey Emeth." In fact, an alternate address for the site is 6124 South May Street.

*Southside Hebrew Congregation*
*7359 South Chappel Avenue (at East 74th St) | 60649*

If you didn't know better, you might think this building is still used as a synagogue, what with the multiple pieces of remaining Judaica that are visible. (The subtle "AN" in a circle is the main clue to its different status. It stands for All Nations Worship Assembly.) Especially on the side street there are many remaining Jewish stars, stained glass windows, and Jewish clues. The Ten Commandments is written in Hebrew inside a single tablet near the roofline. Each of the three front doors has part of the history of the congregation rendered in English: "Ohavei Emunah" and "The South-Side Hebrew Congregation" and "Etz Hayyim" still remain as tributes. The building appears to be in very good condition. The American Synagogue Directory of 1960 states that Rabbi Maurice I. Kliers and President Louis Rosenstein were their leaders.

Southside Hebrew Congregation (Conservative) South Shore neighborhood. SSHC was founded in the 1880s and moved to the South Shore community in 1927 where they merged with Etz Hayyim and Ohave Emunah. The synagogue was designed by Chicago architect Morris Komar in 1926. They moved to Chicago's Gold Coast in the 1970s.

*Congregation Bikur Cholim*
*8927 South Houston Avenue | 60617*

The design of this midblock brick former synagogue is somewhat different from others in the Windy City. The two towers, topped by domes, are a remarkable feature. The decorative scalloping on each tower and near the roofline of the main section of the building are quite nice. Above the arched entrance we can still read in English "Congregation" and "Chicago" but the rest of the name was detached (and the remainder is sloppy). But in Hebrew the name and a famous biblical quote are quite clear: the *Ma Tovu* ("How Goodly" prayer) from Numbers 24 in the Torah. Beneath that is the name "Bet HaKnesset Bikur Cholim" and below that, the Hebrew and English years. It is still a pretty building and in use as a church. Sometime after 2011, according to Google Maps, the Jewish stars that were on the front gate were removed.

Agudath Achim- Bikur Cholim (Orthodox), originally Bikur Cholim, was founded in 1889, the iconic synagogue built in 1898. Later as the original members' families moved away and their ranks began to dwindle, Beth

Sholom B'nai Zaken Ethiopian Hebrew Congregation shared this sacred space. In 2003, the Congregation elected to put the building up for sale, and purchased the former Lawn Manor Beth Jacob at 66th Street and Kedzie Avenue.

# Former Synagogues in Ohio: Cleveland and Suburbs, Toledo, and Lorain

Ohio has been home to notable Jewish communities, and I documented synagogues in the state on two separate occasions. My main focus has been Cleveland, followed by a few smaller urban and suburban areas.My first visit to Cleveland was in the summer of 2014, with my older daughter, and my second was in early July 2023. During the 2023 trip I also visited Toledo, Sandusky and Lorain. (This second trip was directly after my visit to Detroit.)

In 2014 I spent one morning driving around to find former synagogues, most clustered in an extended neighborhood, but it was difficult navigating around some sections because a major street and certain smaller roads were undergoing extensive renovations. (There were multiple trucks and workers throughout those roads.) I did not deal with that issue in 2023 when I traversed a larger segment of Cleveland, and even found three former synagogues by chance. During the second trip I also revisited a few I had seen previously, and was able to visit inside one on Cedar Avenue. One of the most helpful resources I used was Jewish History of Cleveland, a collection of nine detailed neighborhood maps.

That was actually an awkward experience, inadvertently. I saw a man sitting in a chair on the landing of one former synagogue now being used as a church. I parked my car and walked up the stairs, spoke with him and he was friendly. He let me inside and said to feel free to snap photographs. As I walked around the main sanctuary, I spied a corpse in an open casket. The man continued to speak with me so, to be cordial, I continued to do so as well. This was not the first time I had ever entered a former synagogue, being used as a church, and noticed that a casket was present (the other time was in the old B'nai Jeshurun on MLK Jr. Boulevard in Newark).

## CLEVELAND

*Chebra Agudath Achim*
*6411 Quincy Avenue (near East 64th Street) | 44104*

A modest-sized former synagogue, this mottled brick building is a basic box style, and no Judaica seems to be visible. The congregation bought this property in 1917, but they actually incorporated earlier, in 1891, and resided elsewhere before Quincey Avenue. This building did not last long as a shul; they left in 1929 and by 1931 the first of three consecutive churches moved in.The Jewish congregation merged into the Taylor Road Synagogue in the early 1950s. They are part of the Mount Olive Cemetery in Solon, Ohio.

*Euclid Avenue Temple*
*8206 Euclid Avenue (at East 82nd Street) | 44103*

There are large synagogues, and there are occasional huge ones. The former Euclid Avenue Temple is one of the largest former synagogues in Cleveland, an impressive campus of dark brown brick buildings. It's hard to see the sizable dome on top unless you look from a few blocks away. As big as it is, the beautiful details are still worth seeking out as you examine this fortress-like construction. The varying patterns of brick, the different sizes and types of windows, all make for a very impressive place. Some of those patterns are subtle Jewish stars. If you can get inside to see the main sanctuary, do so. It is beautiful and has some of the original synagogue memorial windows. The Hebrew name of the congregation is Anshe Chesed and the architect for this grand structure was Israel Lehman. The sanctuary has stained glass windows designed by Louis Tiffany. The synagogue was also known familiarly as Brickner's Temple, after their longtime rabbi Barnett Brickner. In 1957 they moved to Beachwood and became known as Anshe Chesed Fairmount Temple. But then in 2024 they merged with The Temple-Tifereth Israel and are now called Mishkan Or.

*Ohave Emuno*
*7115 (7) Cedar Avenue | 44103*

There isn't any overt Judaica on the exterior of this brick former synagogue, but if you look carefully at two second floor stained glass windows, you can see that they did have Jewish stars, which have been altered. The congregation met here from 1923–1938. Earlier their name was Ohavei Emuna.

*Cleveland Jewish Center*
*1117 East 105th Street (at Grantwood Avenue) | 44108*

Some of Cleveland's former synagogues seem to have little or no Jewish identifiers, but the former Cleveland JC has a wealth of them. It certainly looks like it is still an active Jewish institution. The Hebrew names used here were Anshe Emeth- Beth Tefilo and the building was used by the Center from 1920–1950. This is a large brick building, just a block away from Shaaray Torah, with neoclassical details and a thorough tribute to Jewish life through the centuries. One of the most remarkable aspects is the list of Jewish luminaries posted above the second floor windows: they include Moses,the prophets Isaiah, Jeremiah, Ezekiel, Amos, Hosea, Ezra, Nehemiah, Hillel, Jehudah Hanassi, Saadia, Maimonides, Jehudah Halevi, Rashi. At the grand main entrance, which includes three sets of double doors and four massive columns, there is also a set of Lions of Judah with a Decalogue. There is also an eight-word phrase in Hebrew, not typically posted on the exterior of a synagogue, from Psalm 29: *Havu la'adonai kavod shemo, hishtachavu la'adonai be'hadrat kodesh* (worship the Lord in the beauty of holiness). The building appears to be in good condition, and the church there now has only placed a few discrete signs on the campus. This impressive site has a 2,400 seat auditorium, an indoor pool and a gym.

*Tifereth Israel (Wilson Avenue Temple)*
*5600 Central Avenue | 44104*

This huge former synagogue, sitting on the corner of two large streets, is like a fortress, and dates to the 1890s. It was actually referred to as the Wilson Avenue Temple, not just Tifereth Israel (Wilson Avenue is the former name of East 55th Street.) Sporting a few shades of brown, the complex was designed by Lehman and Schmitt, who also designed the Euclid Avenue Temple. Later they moved to the East 105th Street site. Officially the congregation was here from 1894–1924.

*Tifereth Israel*
*1855 East 105th Street | 44106*

Established in 1850, Tifereth Israel is the city's second oldest Jewish congregation. This wonderful building, nearby the Cleveland Museum of Art and large public gardens, has many beautiful details on the building and the grounds. It is on the National Register of Historic Places, and thus has been well preserved, even if it is no longer housing a Reform synagogue.

Where does one start to appreciate this building? By gazing at the dome above the main sanctuary? At the three-door main entrance? The main pretty windows, or the arch on the main street? There are several Jewish stars throughout. Built in 1924, it seems indestructible.

Since the days of the synagogue it has been a performing arts center and a charter school.

The congregation moved in the late 1960s to Beachwood and is still located there, although as of 2024 they merged with another long-standing congregation and became Mishkan Or.

*Shaaray Torah/Beth Israel/Beth Hamedrash Hagadol*
*1161 East 105th Street | 44108*

The former synagogue has a nice appearance, a red brick building with three doors, four columns, five lancet windows and two stars on the front. However, those two stars each have five points, not six as would a Jewish star. There doesn't seem to be any real remaining Judaica here.

*Oer Chodosh | 10522 Amor Avenue | 44108*

This mottled brick former synagogue has had changes made to it, and there are just two small clues to its Jewish past. There is a small cornerstone far to the left and another far to the right of the main entrance, and each shares data about this site. The one to the right of the doors has the Hebrew name of the shul, Oer Chodosh, Anshe Sfard. The one on the left seems to have the dedication date, but it has been painted over many times. A large circular window is long gone, bricked in. The congregation goes back to 1894 but experienced a split in 1919. They resided here from 1922–1949. In the 1950s they moved to University Heights, and closed in the late 1990s.

*Tetiever Ahavath Achim Anshe Sfard*
*954 Linn Drive | 44108*

This former synagogue had a long name for a smallish, brick box building. There is a three-part front, nicely balanced, but there doesn't seem to be any remaining Judaica. There are places where the Judaica likely appeared: cornerstones that have been smoothed over, and above the main doors you can just make out the ghosting of Hebrew letters and two Jewish stars. The congregation merged with others and lives on elsewhere. They worshiped here from 1926–1954.

*N'vai Zedek Congregation*
*11901 Union Avenue (at East 119th Street) | 44105*

This former synagogue of brick was designed by Meyer Altshuild, according to Cleveland Jewish History. Aside from a faded cornerstone, no Judaica seems to be visible on the exterior, but the building and certain details are reminiscent of many early 20th century synagogue buildings. Rabbi Eliezer Feldberger led the congregation according to the American Synagogue Directory of 1960. A previous address for the congregation was 3386 East 119th Street. They worshiped here from 1923–1957. They merged into the Warrensville Center Synagogue in 1959.

*Ohel Jacob*
*3473 East 140th Street | 44120*

This modest, boxy brick former synagogue has retained a number of identifiers from its Jewish past. From top to bottom, there is still a small cast stone Jewish star medallion at the peak, and a few feet below that is a small sign reading "1925." Just below that is a stained glass window with a Jewish star, and two other small Jewish stars at the far ends of the building front. Below the window there is a sign with the shul name in Hebrew, although it is small and some of the words are difficult to read. "Congregation [something] Ohel Jacob Anshe Sfard". Two white cornerstones seem to have had their writing rubbed out.

## TOLEDO

*The Temple*
*2335 Collingwood Boulevard (between Acklin Avenue & Winthrop Street) | 43620*

Spanning a full block, with large lawns and a bold entrance, the complex once known as The Temple almost seems like a small college campus. It sits one block over from a large church of a similar sprawling style. The Temple is of sandy brick and the name is still easily seen in cast stone, near the roofline. The entrance has five arches and doorways and four columns. Glimpse at the main building from the Winthrop Street side and see the dome. The school entrance on Winthrop still has "The Temple" emblazoned above the doors, and a stone that reads "Congregation Shomer Emunim Founded 1875" and the Hebrew date. The Acklin Avenue side has a pretty stone Jewish star above the entrance. Overall an impressive site and sight. In the American Synagogue Directory of 1960 their listing includes Rabbi Leon Israel Fever, Associate Rabbi Stephen A. Schafer and President Edward B. Arenson. This building is now used by a church, and the Jewish congregation moved to the nearby suburb of Sylvania.

*B'nai Israel*
*2146 North 12th Street (at Bancroft Street) | 43620*

This reddish-brown brick, two building complex is stately and pretty, with several remaining stained glass windows from the synagogue. There is a plain Decalogue above the main entrance, but perhaps the more intriguing feature is the set of unusually shaped windows right above the three doors. The rear of the main sanctuary, as seen from North Street (and the parking lot) has another set of atypical windows, almost echoing the design on the front of the building. This is clever and I cannot remember seeing something quite like this elsewhere. On the Bancroft Street side, there is a window with a pretty menorah design in it. The other building (school, etc.) is just a touch less dramatic, with a sign above the doors that reads "This arch dedicated to memory of Dr. Julius H. Jacobson." On the Bancroft Street side there are more pretty stained glass windows, one of which features a pretty menorah. The building is on the National Register of Historic Places. They began as an Orthodox group and became Conservative later. They are now located in nearby Sylvania.

## LORAIN

*Agudath B'nai Israel*
*299 West 9th Street (at Reid Avenue) | 44052*

This is one of the more heartbreaking sites, in my opinion. It was rainy when I approached, and I waited for a break in the precipitation in order to take worthy photographs. This is a spacious, regal former synagogue with a large dome, a beautiful floral rose window with a Jewish star in the center, and many gorgeous details. A Byzantine styled, castle-like structure, it was a shul, then became a church in the 1970s, but when I visited it sat vacant. Their first service was in 1925. "ABI" was the result of three separate congregations merging as one. Back in the American Synagogue Directory of 1960 they were led by Rabbi Samuel Meyer and President Isadore Jacobs. They are now located elsewhere in Lorain, on Meister Road.

# Former Synagogues in Detroit

Detroit is celebrated for its major role in the automobile production industry, and for its large part in the history of pop music. It also earned an unfortunate reputation for its vast urban decay. It is less well known for having had one of the largest midwestern Jewish communities, but there are many former synagogues to be found throughout the Motor City.

The reason I found out initially about the importance of Detroit to Jewish American history, was from a fascinating website called *Shtetlhood*, Lost Synagogues of Detroit (shtetlhood.com) In 2006 when I was setting up my exhibition of black and white photographs of Brooklyn's lost synagogues, at the Brooklyn Historical Society, I began to think about former synagogues in other American cities. Searching online I found a website devoted to former shuls in the Bronx, and then one focused on Detroit's former synagogues.

Another helpful resource was the Facebook page "Historical Detroit Area Architecture". The many postings by Benjamin Gravel include intriguing data and other people have added worthy commentary.

I visited Detroit in early July 2023, starting my day in northern New York State, driving west through Pennsylvania and Ohio, then arriving in Michigan in the early evening. After stopping by the Motown Museum (which had closed fifteen minutes before I arrived), I began driving to the locations of former synagogues, using addresses from *Shtetlhood*, the 1920–21 American Jewish Yearbook, American Synagogue Directory, and other, more recent sources.

Many of the buildings that I saw dated to the 1920s, but others were older while others were from the post World War Two era. A sizable number were large, stately buildings, while others were more modest. Most are being used now as churches or for schools, and a few sit empty. Some appear to be in great shape from outside, while others are rotting away, the floors and walls falling apart.

To me, Detroit in 2023 was an eye-opening mix of deterioration and renovation, well-maintained areas and blocks of desolation. Some former synagogues were surrounded by overgrown, grassy lots while others anchored thriving street corners. A few stand on major roads while many are found on smaller, largely residential streets.

To an extent the former synagogues and conditions of Detroit reminded me of the two times I had visited Camden, New Jersey, but the contrasts were greater here. I had also seen this juxtaposition in Buffalo and Rochester, in New York, but in Detroit it was more dramatic.

I also drove around the downtown region and the area near Wayne State University, and was struck by the past and present grandeur of Detroit as well.

The former synagogues that I saw do not add up to the full amount of synagogue buildings that have stood in Detroit; in so many parts of Detroit there are buildings that are gone, and I realized that I saw an incomplete set of sites. Still, I was able to get a good sense of this once sizable and vibrant Jewish community.

The zip code with the most former synagogues to see is 48206, which includes Dexter-Linwood, Jamison, and Wildemere Park. The Motown Museum is located in the southeast tip of the zip code (and I was thrilled to stop by). I located eleven former shuls here. The next most "populous" for lost synagogues was 48202, just east of 48206. Prominent Woodward Avenue bisects this zip code area, and the Cultural Center is in the southern segment.

There is one active synagogue in downtown Detroit and I drove by it, and parked near it to eat dinner. The next day I spent hours driving around and documenting former synagogues. The most haunting one was on Blaine Street, a once-pretty brick building that is now empty and crumbling. Sadly, their active congregation, the Isaac Agree Downtown Synagogue, was in the news for a horrid reason when their president Samantha Woll was murdered in late 2023.

As I explored Detroit, I kept in mind the words of a man I had met earlier in 2023, at a luncheon on Purim. An Orthodox Jewish family in my neighborhood had invited me for a lavish meal in their home, and shortly after I arrived, I fell into conversation with one of their older family members. He had grown up in Detroit (and had not been as religiously observant when young) and he shared with me many thoughtful memories of his earlier days in the city. He stressed, more than once, that it had been a large and warm Jewish community and he wanted me to know of its illustrious past.

*Tushiyah United Hebrew School*
*609 East Kirby Street (at St. Antoine Street) | 48202*

This sizable brick corner building could still be mistaken for the Hebrew school it was built as, since its name is clearly seen in a panel above the main doors. The most interesting aspect of this pleasantly designed structure is the streamlined gable with embedded urns, two Jewish stars and a menorah. There are a few other carved pieces and brick outcroppings that look nice here. As per the 2013 Google map images, many of the windows were boarded up, and now there are modern windows installed. It was converted to residential use in 2018. It is located near the Detroit Institute of Arts. The building was designed by Isadore M. Lewis, and opened in 1922. After the School moved out, a church came in, and later it was used in a few other manners. It was placed on the National Register of Historic Places in 2011.

*Temple Beth El*
*8801 Woodward Avenue (at Gladstone Avenue) | 48202*

Anchoring the corner of a major street, across from an old church, the former Temple Beth El is a formidable neo-classical structure. Take in the six thick Ionic columns as well as two pilasters; three large doors; "Temple Beth El" still visible in English on the front, and on the side street "My House Shall Be Called The House of Prayer For All People." This quote from the prophet Isaiah is also popular with Christian congregations. The building seems to be in good condition except for the front steps, which have noticeable wear and tear. The building was designed in 1922 by Albert Kahn, who was also a member of the congregation. The construction company used was Brayton Engineering Company. Beth El was here through 1973 and then moved to suburban Bloomfield. The American Synagogue Directory of 1960 lists Rabbi Dr. Richard C. Hertz and President Philip R. Marcuse as their leaders.

*Owen Shul*

*586–88 Owen Avenue | 48202*

Located in the middle of a lengthy block, this post World War Two building is boxy and the one stylistic element that makes it special is the set of abstract windows, thin vertical bands stretching from top to bottom. Formally it was known as Beth Moses. A church is now housed here.

*Beth David*
*2201 Elmhurst Street (at 14th Street) | 48206*

This stately corner building is large and a bit forbidding. The English name "BETH DAVID" (bisected by a Decalogue) remains intact, as do a few Jewish stars and menorah designs on the front and side of the building. The church that is there now added a lawn sign and a cornerstone, but otherwise it looks quite like a synagogue. Among the other appealing touches are two griffins that flock the main entrance arch. And on the back of the building there is a pretty set of five windows.There is an interesting, humbling artifact in the Yeshiva University Library archives that pertains to this congregation: a paper titled "COME ONE AND ALL To Witness This Historic Occassion (sic) Transfer of Sifrei Torah to New Building (and start of all services) Sunday, March 23, 1958." From this we learn when the congregation moved out.

This building was designed by John L. Popkin, built in 1927–28, and was also known as B'nai David. Among their clergy were Rabbi Joshua Sperka and Cantor Chaim Adler.

*Aaron Israel*
*2565 Elmhurst Street (at Linwood Street) | 48206*

This modest red brick building on a corner has one remaining Jewish star near the roofline.

It was called the Stoliner Shul because the people who founded the shul were from Stolin, Russia. According to Shtetlhood, "it was built (in the 1920s) for the followers of the Stoliner rebbe, Reb Yaakov Perlov, who came annually from Williamsburg, Brooklyn, to lead services for a week after Passover." The rebbe died in Detroit and was buried here. An alternate name for the synagogue was Bais Aaron v'Isroel. The building was in the news in August 2024 when noted klezmer musician and historian Yale Strom and his band Hot Pstromi played a concert in the former shul-church, dubbed "Hallelujahs in the House: A Celebration of Gospel and Khasidic Music" Strom is from Detroit and members of his family worshipped at this synagogue.

*Nusach Hari*
*12100 Holmur Street (at Duane Street) | 48206*

This boxy pale brick building, with a streamlined, chiseled entrance, features two signs that reveal its original life as a synagogue. The upper one is "In Memory Of" someone in Hebrew on the left, English on the right. But it is difficult to read fully because it has been marred. The lower sign has larger Hebrew words above, English below. But this too is not easy to read, save for the section "CONGREGATION NUSACH HARI." The church there now bricked up a few windows and added crosses and a sign. A famous rabbi, the Frierdiker Rebbe, came to visit the congregation in 1930. The congregation had Lubavticher roots.

*Beth Schmuel*
*12837 Dexter Avenue (at Buena Vista Street) | 48206*

This is an oddly segmented, spread out building; the eye-catching element is a Biblical quote rendered in English as "Thou shalt love thy neighbor as thyself" in capital letters. Next to this, set in two lines, is something clumsily spackled over– with a bit of inspection it is the Hebrew version, *V'ahavta L'reacha Kamocha* and a Jewish star. Another more subtle remnant from the synagogue days is the main entrance, with four doors and twelve panels (representing the Twelve Tribes). The building is on a corner, with a sizable parking lot adjacent to it. According to the American Synagogue Directory of 1960, their rabbi was Joseph Rabinowitz and their president was Isador Rosenberg. Rabbi Rabinowitz founded the congregation in 1926, and the Dexter Avenue building was erected in 1948 and they remained here until 1959. After this congregation left, Dovid Ben Nuchim moved in and stayed until 1965. The Rabbi made aliyah to Israel and established a new congregation with the Beth Schmuel name (with the Detroit members' permission). Dovid Ben Nochim is still active in Oak Park.

*B'nai Moshe*

*11359 Dexter Avenue (at Lawrence Street) | 48206*

The name of this former synagogue is still emblazoned on the front of the building, in a slightly novel manner: a Decalogue splits a pair of circles, one with the name "B'nai" and the other "Moshe" in Hebrew. This neo-classically styled corner building sports five handsome doors at the entrance, and several pretty stained glass windows on the front and Lawrence Street side, many with Jewish stars remaining. The building was designed by Kohner & Payne, and built in 1928–1929. On the Shtethood site, Anne Klarman Kelz recalled that "When the congregation first began, the meeting records were written in Hungarian." Another former member recalled that they had Boy Scouting here. Among the clergy that served here were Rabbi Lehrman, and Louis Klein was a cantor. The congregation moved two more times and is still active, but in nearby West Bloomfield.

*B'nai Zion*
*3836 Humphrey Street (at Holmur Street) | 48206*

B'nai Zion is one of several former Detroit shuls whose name is still visible on the exterior of the building, although in this case it is harder to see. In a circle near the roofline there is a cast stone decoration that has the name in both Hebrew and English. Two other smaller circles near the roofline also have Hebrew lettering. In addition there are three Jewish stars on the front of the building. The Holmur Street side features several nice windows. This may be a medium-sized , fairly modest structure but these touches and other details give it a classy look.

Also called the Humphrey Shul, they had a Young Couples Minyan. We learn from the American Synagogue Directory of 1960 that Rabbi Solomon H. Gruskin and President Morris Snow were their leaders.

*Shaarey Zedek/Hank Greenberg shul*
*2900 Chicago Boulevard (at Lawton Street) | 48206*

Set back from the corner of Chicago and Lawton, the former Shaarey Zedek is across from a well-kept boulevard with a grassy mall in the middle. Large and fortress-like, with brown brick and cast stone striping, this building is impressive and still has Judaica on display. A Jewish star, two menorahs and a Decalogue are nicely maintained, and the Lawton Street side has lovely windows. The School Building is also on the Lawton side. The complex is so large that it backs onto the next street, Rochester Street. The quirky claim to fame for this synagogue was that the future Baseball Hall of Famer Hank Greenberg, star player for the Detroit Tigers, attended Yom Kippur services here instead of playing in an important game. (He had earlier played in the games held on Rosh HaShanah.) The American Synagogue Directory of 1960 lists their rabbi as Morris Adler and their president as Abraham Satovsky. Other clergy over their years included Rabbi Irwin Groner and Cantor Jacob Sonenklar. Among the activities held here were Cub Scouting. The congregation was established in 1861 and had an earlier home, long since demolished. The land for this Chicago Boulevard building was purchased from the Archdiocese of Detroit. The congregation lives on, in suburban West Bloomfield.

*Jewish Free Burial Society/Hebrew Benevolent Society*
*2995 Joy Road | 48206*

The front of this boxy brick building is a kind of atypical design for Detroit, with a touch of whimsy. Perhaps it could be described as futuristic or vaguely Mediterranean, mixed with Art Deco. Also look carefully for the two Jewish stars, on each side of the front, that seem to have been partially sanded down. In the American Synagogue Directory of 1960 we learn that their Executive Director was Rabbi Israel I. Rockove and their President was Nathan P. Rossen.

According to the Historical Detroit Area Architecture page on Facebook, the building was designed by Maurice H. Finkel and built in 1930. The Hebrew name was Chesed Shel Emes. Originally incorporated in 1916, it is now known as Hebrew Memorial Chapel and located elsewhere.

*Beth Emmanuel/Taylor Shul*
*1550 Taylor Street (at Woodrow Wilson Street) | 48206*

This corner brick building is somewhat large, not too remarkable, and does not seem to have any remaining Judaica, except a hint of a Decalogue (now mostly covered) in the front.There is still a small cornerstone that reads "1924" and just on the other side of it a Hebrew year number seems to have been scratched out. The church there now added two portrait murals and an additional building on the side. At least up until 2013, according to Google Maps, the windows were of colored glass panels, and the building was somewhat more shabby. Modern windows and a cleanup have given the site a better look overall. According to DetroitUrbex, it was formally Congregation Beth Tefilo Emmanuel and built in 1924. A church bought the building in the early 1960s but they closed down in 2012. Another group moved in later on.The shul moved to Southfield. Among the clergy who served here was Cantor Boyarsky in the 1930s.

*Beth Yehuda*
*1600 Pingree Street (at Woodrow Wilson Street) | 48206*

This brick corner building (sandy brick on the entrance and one side, brownish brick on the other side) has been shorn of any obvious Judaica. It has a few interesting stylistic touches, with artsy arching over a few windows. People reminisced on Shtetlhood that "this was the site of Beth Yehuda from 1932–1944" and "It moved (elsewhere) where it merged and is called B'nai Israel Beth Yehudah."

*Mishkan Yisroel*
*2627 Blaine Street (near Linwood Street) | 48206*

Perhaps the most forlorn former synagogue I encountered in Detroit was this small brick site. Decades ago it must have been pretty, with nice windows and a still-remaining Jewish star and split Decalogue near the roofline. But according to Google Maps, at least going back to 2007, it has been abandoned and overgrown. A church resided here years ago but now even that sign is gone. I walked around to the back and looked inside, to see a mostly rotted-out interior. According to the Detroit Facebook page, the building dates to 1925. In 1958 the congregation moved elsewhere and this building was sold to a church. On the Shtetlhood site someone reminisced that his family attended "the Blaine Shul with my grandfather" (it was often called by the street name). Rabbi Stollman officiated here.

*Avas Achim/Delmar Shul*
*9243 Delmar Street (at Westminster Street) | 48211*

This once medium-sized brick building has seen various additions, so that it is now part of a nearly full-block complex. The church there now has kept a few reminders of the Jewish past, such as four Jewish stars spread out by the entrance level, and another Jewish star above the three front doors, According to Google Maps, up until at least 2013 there was also a much smaller building directly across the street, with a Jewish star above the door. The main building was designed by Maurice H. Finkel and built in 1917. It was an Orthodox congregation. According to Shtetlhood, the shul was often called "Avas Achim," a shortened version of the actual name Ahavas Achim. In the late 1960s it merged with Beth Aaron, and they merged into Adat Shalom in the late 1990s.

*Ahavath Zion*
*446 Holbrook Avenue (near Beaubien Boulevard) | 48202*

In several ways, the former Ahavath Zion is similar to other Detroit former synagogues. It is near a corner, it is brick faced, it has a moderate size. It also has its name written in English, "Cong. Ahavath Zion," near the roofline. It also has a menorah and Jewish star design over the main door, and few Jewish stars on the front (although one has mostly crumbled). What makes this lost synagogue a bit different are some of the intricate details of stone, and stained glass windows that have panache. Even on the sides of the building you can see several original windows. (Others have been replaced.) The building was designed by Kohner & Seeler, and built 1921–22. According to Shtetlhood, "The congregation was almost entirely immigrant Jews from southeastern Poland" and their families.

*Temple Beth-El*
*3424 Woodward Avenue (near Eliot Street) | 48201*

This earlier location of Beth-El is of a different classical style (especially the large dome) than the later building, also on Woodward. It is a striking building as well, and has led an intriguing life from its days as a house of worship, a theater, (the Bonstelle Theatre) part of the Wayne Street University, and future ambitious plans. It served Beth-El from 1903 to 1922 and was designed by member Albert Kahn. Rabbi Leo M. Franklin was their rabbi at this time.

*B'nai Israel*

*582 East Ferry Street | 48202*

The former B'nai Israel building, of orangey brick, has a style that is quite similar to former synagogues I have seen in parts of New York City and urban New Jersey. It's a modest size, with three distinct sections (I call this the "open Torah" style) and although not elaborate, it has nice elements. There is a split Decalogue, one tablet gracing the top of each outer section. Five thin windows on the upper level have charm, and there is a Jewish star (albeit partly covered over or dismantled) above the main entrance, in a half-rose window. The building was designed by Isadore M. Lewis and built in 1922.

*Beth Abraham*
*12517 Linwood Street | 48206*

Charming but disheveled, the former Congregation Beth Abraham retains an etched sign with its name in English, as well as a split Decalogue, from its synagogue days. The pretty brickwork and other details give it a special look. (I confess this was one of my favorite Detroit sites.) But the building needs repairs and touch up in order to return to its true former glory. Searching through Google Maps, you can see that in 2017 there was another building besides it, not a grassy lawn. A church now occupies the space. According to Shtetlhood, people recalled that "the Shamas (caretaker) of the shul in the late 40's-early 50's was a gentleman by the name of Mr. Landgarten." "Originally the congregation met in someone's house in the early 1890s." It was also known as a "Galitzianer shul." The congregation later moved to 8100 West 7 Mile Road; and that site became a church too.

*Cong. Adas/Adath Yeshurun*
*2625 Tyler Street | 48238*

When I stopped by this plain red brick building, I noticed two things quickly: a sign over the doorway that read "CONGREGATION ADAS YESHURUN" and the lack of other buildings on this block. (I also saw the small cornerstone that read "1926".) But when searching other years on Google Maps, I saw that this street had several more houses just a few years ago. Another church occupied this building and had left a Jewish star visible, further above the doorway. "Called the Tyler Shul by all who went here" wrote someone on Shtetlhood.

*Beth Moses*
*13925 Linwood Street (at Oakman Court) | 48238*

The cornerstone of this post-WW2 building reads "Beth Moses Founded 1902 Erected 1950" but above this is a sign for the Mt. Lebanon Baptist Church. This brick building is not remarkable but this cornerstone clue to its past life is a nice reminder. This corner building on a quiet stretch also has a lawn. According to the American Synagogue Directory of 1960 they were led by Rabbi Gerson Frankel and President Julius Halperin.

*Shaarey Torah*
*17750 Brush Street | 48203*

The boxy, rather plain design of the former Shaarey Torah seems special in that it sits on a large plot of land, with no other buildings on either side of it. Assuming there were buildings in the past and they are gone, this former shul is quite the survivor. There are two notable Jewish relics on the front of the building: a small cast stone sign above the doors that reads in Hebrew, "Cong. Shaarey Torah," and a longer, narrower sign in block capital letters in English, near the roofline, that reads "UNITED HEBREW SCHOOLS". Aside from that, the church that is in the building now put out a handful of flower pots on the steps, a nice touch.

*Temple Israel*
*17400 Manderson Road | 48203*

The former Temple Israel campus is palatial: a large, sprawling building with different sections(the rectangular main section with a rounded part at the other end that has the look of an arena). There is a sizable parking lot and lengthy lawns. It has a suburban, not urban feel. And the parking lot is atypical of urban synagogues, certainly. At the main entrance above the doors is chiseled in Hebrew *Emet Dayan Shalom*. Overall this is a handsome complex, a far cry from some of the small, simple house shuls in the inner city of Detroit.The architect was William E. Kapp. We learn from the American Synagogue Directory of 1960 that they were helmed by Rabbi Dr. Leon Fram and President Louis H. Schostak. This was one of the last Reform synagogues in Detroit. The congregation moved to West Bloomfield.

*Beth Aaron*
*18000 Wyoming Avenue | 48221*

If you read Hebrew, stand at the entrance to this lengthy, one-story building and you will read "Bet HaKnesset Bet Aharon." But that Jewish congregation is long gone, and a church is in its place. Although most of this building is not remarkable, the main entrance has a special flare, with its chiseled Hebrew name sign and a two-part Twelve Tribes of Israel motif (six panels on each side of the entrance). Two sets of dark windows are another nice touch. Aside from the church sign, this site is still dominated by its Judaic past. The American Synagogue Directory of 1960 states that their rabbi was Benjamin H. Gorrelick and their president was William I. Liberson. The building was designed by Louis Redstone and built in 1951.

# Former Baltimore Synagogues

Baltimore is a large harbor town known for its importance in early American history, for its baseball and football teams, for its proximity to the nation's capital, for its more recent years of urban decay and crime, and for its cultural and educational institutions. It also has importance as far as urban American Jewish life. The Jewish community of Baltimore has shifted its locales, and while there are a few dozen active synagogues in Baltimore and nearby suburbs, there are also nearly twenty former synagogues. A key year in the community's history is 1880, when the city had a population of around 10,000 Jews. And by 1920 the number was over 65,000.

The former synagogues tend to be in the north and west sections of the city, with several not far from the Maryland Zoo. The condition of these lost synagogue buildings runs the gamut from nice to abandoned and falling apart. Most are now used as churches and a few have other purposes.

I visited Baltimore twice to see former synagogues; first in the springtime of 2018 and the second time in early January 2024. Initially I only found a few, because the main reason for my visit was to visit musical instrument stores, for a website article I wrote. At the time I also stopped by the famous Lloyd Street Synagogue, which has been used as a museum for many years. In 2024 my trip amounted to a few hours of driving around to see 17 synagogues, two of which I had seen in 2018 as well. I did notice that one of those two buildings had a For Sale sign on the front, and the other seemed to have been cleaned up.

These buildings ranged from modest pre-World War Two buildings to large, elaborate structures. Some are situated on streets that have a few or even many abandoned and disheveled buildings. I did not actually expect this. Others are located in better maintained neighborhoods. The names of most of these congregations are similar to those found in other cities and towns in the US (such as Anshe Sfard, Shaarei Zion, B'nai Jacob) but a few had Baltimore as part of their name.

*Anshe Sfard*
*4 North Broadway | 21231*

This modest grayish brick building, situated on a corner, is notable for its pairs of lancet windows, large and small. It is set on a steep street and has an angled bottom; I have seen a few other former synagogues arranged this way, such as in the Bronx. Judaic details on the front of the building include a Decalogue, and most importantly, a sign in Hebrew which reads "Congregation Anshe Sfard" (although some of the letters are not as clear as others). It was in decent condition as Lamb of Life Baptist Church when I visited in 2018, and still looks good, but as of January 2024, the building sports a "For Sale" sign. According to Kenny Friedman on the Facebook page "Baltimore Synagogues: Then and Now," the shul was at 4 North Broadway from 1937–1951, but its origins date back to 1887. An earlier address was Aisquith Street. It later merged with other congregations such as Ohr Knesseth Israel, but sadly, it was dissolved in the early 1990s. The archives were donated to the Jewish Museum of Maryland.

*Petach Tikvah*
*5103 Denmore Avenue | 21215*

This post-World War 2 structure is a streamlined, boxy building on a corner that has one particularly nice piece of remaining Judaica: a large window paneled Jewish star over the main entrance. The star is now partly covered by the current church's sign. This kind of simple, boxy design is reminiscent of former (and active) synagogues in parts of New York City and upstate New York, and elsewhere. Kilduffs lists an alternative spelling of the name as "Pethacj Tikuak." This building was a shul from 1950 to 1971. An article in The Sun, dated September 8, 1976, "Landmark Synagogue for Sale" discussed its "being sold because of dwindling membership and changes in the character of the neighborhood." The rabbi then was Rabbi Benjamin G. Axelman and the shul president was William Radin.

*Beth Israel/Lubawitz Nusach Ari*
*2620 Quantico Avenue | 21215*

It's hard to tell how much modification was done by the current owner of this former synagogue, but it does seem hodgepodge. On the second floor there are two small windows, seemingly put together like a Decalogue, and each has a small Jewish star. Other than that, this midblock structure does not have much identifying it as a former shul. According to the American Synagogue Directory of 1960, Rabbi Albert Joseph David and President Hyman Danoff were their leaders.

*Amunas Israel/Congregation Moses Montefiore*
*533/5 South Smallwood Street | 21223*

This modest brick building looks forlorn, with most of the window spaces bricked up. It was never meant to be a standout house of worship, but there is pleasing detailing surrounding the windows on the front, and four simple pilasters. Now it is home to a church, but the shul was here from 1894 through the early 1960s.The congregation lives on, in a different location within the city, and other synagogues merged with it.

*Beth Tfiloh*
*3200 Garrison Boulevard | 21216*

Some former synagogues don't seem to be "former." Judaica is still present here, and there don't appear to be any major changes. The former Beth Tefiloh looked that way to me, except for the discrete lawn sign for "Wayland Baptist Church." Otherwise, this large two-building campus consists of a beautiful main building and a smaller secondary structure. Windows at the main entrance still have Jewish stars, and a Decalogue graces the top of the archway. The rusticated stone here is splendid, and the buildings resemble a European landmark. The two domed towers can be seen a distance away. The American Synagogue Directory of 1960 informs us that Rabbi Dr. Samuel Rosenblatt, President Samuel Epstein and Director Howard Shpritz led the congregation. The shul resided here from 1922 through the mid-1960s, and then moved to another city location.

*Adath Yeshurun*
*4651 Pimlico Road | 21215*

This former synagogue is basically a private home that had a synagogue structure attached to the front of it. Aside from its overall awkward look, there are a few stained glass windows (not in great shape) and a Decalogue that was spackled over. Rabbi Simcha Shafran and President William Caplan led the congregation according to the American Synagogue Directory of 1960. Kenny Friedman wrote on Facebook that "It was founded in 1888. On January 23, 1949, (the) Pimlico Road (site) was dedicated. In 1967, the congregation relocated to Old Court Road and Marriott's Lane, becoming Adath Yeshurun, Old Court Synagogue Center. It dedicated its new sanctuary May 25, 1969. It merged with Mogen Abraham in 1974, becoming Adath Yeshurun-Mogen Abraham, Old Court Synagogue Center."

*Beth Yehuda*
*3911 Garrison Boulevard | 21215*

With its brown brick, Brutalist styling, reminiscent of a fortress, and sizable plaza area in front of the main entrance, this former synagogue has a radically different use of space compared to most of the former synagogues in Baltimore, which do not take up as much room nor in such a manner. Beth Yehuda had more of a suburban than urban layout, and there is not much to remind us of its former life as a synagogue. It had an earlier location at 3820 Garrison, and was at 3911 from 1934 through the 1960s and then moved. The American Synagogue Directory of 1960 tells us that Rabbi Jacob Pearlmutter and President Samuel Barber helmed the synagogue. Other congregations later merged into it.

*Shaarei Zion*
*3459 Park Heights Avenue | 21215*

The former Shaarei Zion is a prime example of neo-classical majesty. The portico above the main entrance still has a Decalogue with Hebrew, and a floral sculpture just above. There is a trio of doors and (filled in) circular windows, four Ionic style columns, and other smart elements. The exterior is well kept.The Good Shepherd Baptist Church here now built an additional newer building that is next door. We learn from the American

Synagogue Directory of 1960 that they were led by Rabbi Dr. Israel Tabak and President Jacob Esterson.

*Sharon/Shearith Israel*
*2104 McCullough Street | 21217*

Compared to the Eutaw Place and Madison Avenue Synagogues, the former Sharon/Shearith Israel is simpler and not too fancy, but has similarities that reveal its stately design. It showcases two turrets, one on each side of the entrance, and each side has a tower-like segment. A Decalogue near the roofline has Hebrew writing, and is topped by a small Jewish star. There is a rose window which in the past featured a Jewish star (and a Wikipedia article shows a photo of this, with half the window covered up and half revealing that Magen David). As of 2024 it is in decent shape from the outside, but the glass is gone from most of the windows. There are other pleasing details here, and a contemporary sign that states "M W Zerubbabel Grand Lodge." The American Synagogue Directory of 1960 mentions only a shul president, J.Morton Lehman.

This is the "oldest continually Orthodox synagogue in Baltimore." It seceded from an earlier shul on Howard Street and merged with a smaller congregation. It still exists today and had a few other homes besides McCullough. This building was their home from 1903 to 1958.

*Ahavas/Ahava Achim*
*427 South Pulaski Street | 21223*

This forlorn corner building has been abandoned for quite some time. It was modest and not fancy to start with, but the disheveled status makes it even more woebegone. There doesn't seem to be any remaining Judaica or any other signifiers. What will become of it? When I stopped by I could hear the wail of fire engine sirens and smell smoke in the near distance. Artist Lissa Abrams painted a portrait of this building and it was in an exhibition that was on view at the Baltimore Hebrew Congregation in 2019.

*Eutaw Place Temple/Oheb Shalom*
*1307 Eutaw Place | 21217*

Stately and highly detailed, this large and elaborate building features three domes, the largest with several Jewish stars. There are many windows and overall they appear to be in very good shape. The grand entrance has three arches and three doorways. This building was modeled after the Great Synagogue of Florence, and it conveys Old World elegance. The architect was Joseph Evans Sperry. The block itself is wide and bisected by a grassy mall, and a monument to Francis Scott Key is across from the building. As listed in the American Synagogue Directory of 1960, Rabbi Abraham D. Shaw and President Samuel S. Strouse were their leaders. This was a Reform congregation, built in 1892 as the second home of Oheb Shalom. Oheb Shalom is still active elsewhere in Baltimore and Congregation Har Sinai merged into it.

*Adath Israel*
*2043 East Baltimore Street | 21231*

Sitting on a corner, this medium-sized, neat brick former shul still has a few pieces of remaining Judaica. There are two small cornerstones (one says "1936" and the other "1899"). According to Kilduffs Baltimore Synagogues, the shul was housed here from 1920 through the late 1940s. A Decalogue is near the roofline, above the main entrance. Later they merged with Beth Isaac. Now this building houses a Latino church.

*Har Zion*
*2014 West North Avenue | 21217*

Somewhat compact and midblock, this former synagogue borrows elements of a few different architectural styles. But the prominent aspect is the gorgeous large rose window, featuring a Jewish star and a flower in the middle. Stained glass panels fill the window, and it appears to be well maintained. Beneath that are a trio of pretty lancet windows with stained glass panels. Now used as a church, this is a modest-sized gem. It opened in 1922 and closed by the mid 1950s.

This congregation merged with Tifereth Israel.

*Chofetz Chaim*
*2002 Presbury Street | 21217*

There is not much left of any Judaic interest to this orange brick building, but it seems well kept. The interesting contemporary touch is the four windows with portraits; it is now a building for a national Black fraternity. There were previous addresses and later ones as well. Rabbi Mordechai Rabinowitz (D. 8/26/1957) served here. He was the rabbi of Har Zion Congregation (founded 1915) and then at Chofetz Chaim Congregation (founded by members who left Har Zion Congregation), beginning at 2130 West North Avenue in 1934 until moving into Presbury Street in 1935. In 1949 they moved into 3702 West Rogers Ave. Chofetz Chaim would merge with Adath Bnei Israel in 1960.

*Madison Avenue Synagogue*
*1901 Madison Avenue | 21217*

The very large former Madison Avenue Synagogue is a fantastic, castle-like structure with two domed towers, a wider domed section behind them, and an intricate entrance of three doors, stairs, and a half-circle of delicate windows. It is situated on a corner, and at the edge of the corner is a historic sign with information about the building, but the name "Berea Temple of Seventh Day Adventists" is highlighted. If you look carefully, one noticeable Jewish star on the front is above the main entrance, capping a Decalogue. There are at least 2 other tiny Jewish stars on the front, worked into designs on pillars. It was a shul from 1891 to 1951. Prior to this location it was known as Baltimore Hebrew Congregation and was in the East Baltimore area. The group hired architect Charles Carson to design this building on Madison Avenue.

*Mishkan Israel*
*2245 Madison Avenue | 21217*

Although this building still has an air of former grandeur, overall it seems bleached out and rundown. Many of the windows have been painted over and the arches lack detail. The building has three sections and the middle has three streamlined pilasters. The sole Judaic touch is a simple Decalogue. The building is now home to a church. It was a shul from 1920 through the early 1960s. The American Synagogue Directory of 1960 states that Rabbi Jehiel B. Shohan and President Morris Lott were their leaders. Earlier they were led by Rabbi Marcus and then Rabbi Shoham. The shul closed around 1960. Stanislaus Russell was the architect.

# Former Synagogues in the Western United States, Plus One Southern

San Francisco and Seattle are two cities in the western section of the United States where I found former synagogues. Through reading and research, I located two former synagogues in San Francisco and two in Seattle. I also found two buildings in Las Vegas but they have been modified so greatly and there seems to be no Judaica remaining on their exteriors, so I decided not to include them in this study.

The city I know best of this group is San Francisco. I first traveled to SF in the summer of 1973 for my cousin's bar mitzvah and have visited over a dozen times, at various times of the year. I have visited active synagogues there as well, for religious services and as a tourist, and have driven to a particular lost synagogue a few times over the years (most recently June 2022). That former synagogue building is in a largely residential part of the city and has not changed much whenever I have seen it. I had seen another one years ago, downtown, but it has since been demolished.

There are more than two lost shuls in Seattle but when I visited in August 2019, I only had time to see two of them. One of them was particularly impressive. I did see one other, now used as a school, but it has since been changed greatly so I didn't include it here. I have also included New Orleans in this section. I visited NOLA twice, first as a college student and nearly thirty years later with my family. The former synagogue there has no obvious Judaica but is historically significant. Each of these cities has active synagogues but they have moved around. There are Chabad congregations in these cities, as well as other synagogues. There are cities in other parts of the Western US that have former synagogues but I was fortunate enough to document this select grouping.

## SAN FRANCISCO

*Temple B'nai David*
*3535 19th Street | 94110*

This is a pretty building with lots of noticeable Judaica. Admire the blue painted Jewish stars as well as Jewish stars embedded in windows. Two Jewish stars are featured on the gate in front of the main entrance. Just above the main doors is a Decalogue with Hebrew words. This had been Congregation B'nai David, built in 1908. It was their second home, built after the Fire of 1906. The shul closed in 1978 and was converted to apartments in 1981. In its heyday it even housed a mikvah.

*Bush Street Synagogue*
*1881 Bush Street | 94109*

You might think that you are gazing at a European architectural treasure when you stop by here, but years ago this was the Bush Street Synagogue. On my many visits to SF, I drove past this but at first had no inkling that it had a Jewish history. Designed by Moses J. Lyon and built in 1895, its Hebrew name was Ohabai Shalome. Earlier the congregation worshipped at a site on Mason Street. In the 1930s the building was sold to an Asian group, and has since served Asian-American communities in a few different functions.

## SEATTLE

*Sephardic Bikur Cholim*
*1915 East Fir Street | 98122*

It is heartening to see a former synagogue building with Jewish stars on three out of four sides of the exterior, such as with the former Sephardic Bikur Cholim. Each of the four doors at the main entrance also has a Jewish star on it. Also take notice of the Decalogue above the main entrance. An interesting stylistic quirk of this building is its asymmetry; the main entrance is not in the middle, but more to one side. I have seen this a few times with other lost shuls, and notably with the former Sephardic Jewish Center on 169th Street in the Bronx. According to Google Maps photos, sometime after June 2008, the name of the synagogue was removed from above the entrance, and covered over. This building opened for the High Holidays in 1929, and was designed by William George Brust Jr. It served the community until 1965, when their next home was built on 52nd Avenue.

*Bikur Cholim*
*104 17th Avenue South | 98144*

This majestic former synagogue of sandy-colored brick, anchored on a corner, was built as a synagogue named Bikur Cholim. Designed by Jewish architect B. Marcus Pritica, it echoes a few different classical styles and features a handsome dome. There are some subtle Jewish stars to be seen here and there, and a blank Decalogue near the roofline. For many years it has been used as the Langston Hughes Performing Arts Institute. The congregation is now known as Bikur Cholim Machzikay Hadath and is located on South Morgan Street in Seattle.

## NEW ORLEANS

*Gates of Prayer*
*709 Jackson Avenue | 70130*

This handsome old building of reddish-brown brick may not have Judaica on display, but it does resemble the style of many synagogue buildings in urban areas. This was the second home of Shaarei Tefiloh (Gates of Prayer), the oldest continuous Jewish congregation in Greater New Orleans. The building here was completed in June 1865, and served the congregation into 1920, when they moved to a renovated former church. Originally Orthodox in affiliation, it moved to Reform later on. Rabbi Moise Bergman and Rabbi Dr. Mendel Silber served the congregation during this period. Now the congregation is located in nearby Metairie. But this Jackson Avenue building had been abandoned for many years, before it was renovated into condominiums, according to Professor Samuel Gruber.

# Conclusions, For Now

I HAVE BECOME SO deeply invested in the topic of former synagogues, that I experience FOMO, fear of missing out. I fear missing out on former synagogues in places that I visit once. I fear missing out on former synagogues in places I have not yet visited. I want to see, document and honor these buildings and their people. I experience FOMO even regarding former synagogues I have seen once or twice, but I don't get to see all their changes.

I experience FOMO also because I know there is more information available for practically every former synagogue. For the most part I am only presenting a bit of what can be known. Then again, this is a common nagging feeling for historians, for teachers, and others who care about their particular topic(s) of research.

I hope to visit other former synagogues, especially in cities, towns and states where I have not ventured forth. I realize this topic has a continuing story or set of stories. It may not be the happiest topic, but delving into it is rewarding and helps people to be educated and inspired.

Certainly I appreciate being acknowledged for my work, and I do like to bring more people into the conversation. I do hope that my work also will help to educate people about Judaism in general, and may help to diminish ignorance of Jews and what they hold dear. I pray that there is more understanding and less hatred, and perhaps my work can help with that, too.

In the past I have offered ideas for lesson plans based on studying former synagogues, so I will discuss this again here. Teachers can have students research a particular former synagogue, or a specific neighborhood and its former synagogues. Students can interview congregants and clergy members about their memories of former synagogues. If students notice that their own synagogues have prayer books or plaques from former synagogues, they can do research based on those items. (Flatbush Jewish

Center, for example, has memorial plaques from two former synagogues that were in the vicinity.) Students of religion, architecture and art, urban studies, American history, library science and other areas can use former synagogues as a subject of study.

Folks, go see these buildings. Learn their stories and maybe learn more about your own stories as well. Amen.

# Glossary: Translations for Non-English Words Used in Synagogues Names

THIS LIST WILL FOCUS first on Hebrew words that are used in the names of synagogues and schools. Afterward I will include place-names. Certain names are fairly common, such as Beth El, Beth Israel, Temple Sholom, B'nai Zion; we see synagogues (former as well as active) with these types of names in various places around the United States. There are also variant spellings in English. And then there are synagogues with names reflective of their American locales, such as North West Hebrew Congregation in Chicago or Bayside Jewish Center in Queens.

Achim: Brothers

Adas/Adath/Hadath: Assembly

Agudas/Agudath: Society

Ahavas/Ahavath/Avas: Lovers of

Am: people, nation (as in Beth Am, house of the people)

Anshe/Ansche/Anschei/Anshei/Anshai/Anshi: People of

Atereth: Glory of

Avodas/Avoda: service, work, worship

B'nai/B'nei: Sons of, people of

Beth: House of

Bikur: Visitors, as in Bikur Cholim (visitors of the sick)

Brith/Brit: covenant

Chevra: friends, a society of

Chofetz Chaim: from Psalm 34; name of a famous rabbi

Darchei: ways, paths of

Emmanuel/Emanu-El: Faith in God (also Emunas/Emunath/Amuna/Amunas)

Emeth/Emet/Emes: Truth

Etz Chaim: Tree of Life

Hagadol: the great (as in Beth Hamedrash Hagadol, the great house of prayer-study)

Hamedrash/Hemidrash: house of prayer-study

Har: mountain, hill (Har Zion, mountain of Zion)

Harav: the rabbi

Hessed/Hesed/Chesed: loving kindness

Jeshurun/Yeshurun: another name for the land of Israel

Kenesseth/Kanesses/Haknesses: house of worship, assemblage

Kesser/Kether/Keter: crown

Khal/K'hal/Kehillah/Kehillas: community

Lubavitz/Lubawitz: referring to Chabad-Lubavitch

Midrash: learning portion

Mikro Kodesh: holy assembly

Mishkan/Mishkon: tabernacle

Mishnayos: reference to the Mishnah, the Oral Torah

Ner: lamp, light, candle

Netzach: eternity, strength, victory

Nusach: style of prayer (as in Nusach Sfard, see below)

Nusach Hari/Nusach Ari: following the custom of the famous Rabbi Isaac Luria

N'vai Zedek: oasis of justice

Ohab/Oheb/Ohev/Ohave: lovers of

Ohel: tent, a place

Oer/Ohr: light (as in Ohr Chadash, new light)

Petach Tikvah: a city in Israel, literally the opening of hope

Poras: boughs, branches

Rodeph/Rodfei: pursuers, seekers

Sfard/Sphard: ritual style common to some Hasidic Jews. Not to be confused with Sephardic, Levantine

Shaare/Shaari/Shaarei/Shaaray/Shaarey: gates of

Shalom/Sholom/Scholom: peace

Shamayim/Shomayim: heaven

Sharon: fertile plain

Shearith: Remnant

Schomre/Shomrey/Shomrei:guardians of

Shul/Schul/Schule:Yiddish word for synagogue

Talmud Torah: religious school (Talmud is the Oral Law in Judaism)

Tifereth/Tiferes: praising

Torah/Tora: the Five Books of Moses, the "Old Testament"

Torath/Toras:plural of Torah

Tushiyah: wisdom, being resourceful

Tzedek/Zedek:righteous

Tzemach Tzedek/Zemach Zedek: Hasidic leader's name, Righteous Scion

Yeshiva/Yeshivas/Yeshivat: Jewish school of learning

Zichron: memory, memorial

Zion: the Jewish people

*Male names*

Yehuda> Judah

Moshe> Moses

Yisrael/Yisroel> Israel

Bezalel> biblical name of an architect

Schmuel> Samuel

Yacoff/Yakov> Jacob

*Places and Names*
Berditchev (in Ukraine), Dorum, Fastover, Halbershtam, Kovno (in Lithuania), Kroz, Lemberg (Lviv in Ukraine), Lida (in Belarus), Lubin (in Poland), Pavalatch/Pavolitch, Pinsk (in Belarus), Tetiever (Tetiev in Ukraine), Ticktin (Tykocin), Uziel (an angel in the Old Testament)

# Selected Bibliography

## BOOKS

Philip Birnbaum, translation, *Daily Prayer Book* (Hebrew Publishing Company, New York,1977)

*American Synagogue Directory*, 1960 American synagogue directory, 1960 : Free Download, Borrow, and Streaming : Internet Archive

Cragoe, Carol Davidson, *How To Read Buildings: A crash course in architectural styles* (Rizzoli International Publications Inc., 2008)

Kolodny, Brad, *Seeking Sanctuary: 125 Years of Synagogues on Long Island* (Segulah Press, 2019)

Packer, Robert A.,*Chicago's Forgotten Synagogues* (Arcadia Publishing, 2007)

Preisler, Julian H., *The Synagogues of Central and Western Pennsylvania: A Visual Journey* (Fonthill Media, 2014)

Scherman, Nosson, ed. *The Stone Edition Tanach* (Mesorah Publications, Brooklyn, NY 1996)

## ARTICLES (SELECTED)

WIN: Former South Side Chicago Synagogue to Become Mixed-Use Creative Space—PRESERVATION CHICAGO

American Synagogues Are Closing at a Record Rate and This Retired Judge Is Rescuing Their Stained Glass Windows | Culture | thejewishnews.com Chicago, etc.

BUCKINGHAM PEWS | The Enterprise Companies

Lifestyle Brand FLATS Chicago Reopens Abandoned Synagogue As Micro Apartments

"If the Rebbe Comes to America, America Will Come to Him!" | Anash.org Detroit

Michigan_Jewish_History_1984_01.pdf pages 11–13 Detroit

Detroiturbex.com—Tried Stone Baptist Church / Taylor Shul Detroit

Bethel Community Transformation Center—Historic Detroit

Congregation Adath Israel Middletown merging with Temple B'nai Abraham Meriden CT

https://www.jewishledger.com/2013/11/celebrating-125-years-of-jewish-meriden/

NJ Jewish News article on the "Synagogues of Newark." Opening reception today at 1 pm.

Alphabet shuls | New Jersey Jewish News (two Irvington shuls)

One of Downtown Jersey City's Oldest Churches to Be Converted into Residences | Jersey Digs
The YM-YWHA Movement in Newark From 1877 Birth to End in 1969
News—New Synagogue for Russian Jews—Newark Religion
News—The Scenes in an Orthodox Synagogue—Newark Religion
Merger plans for Garden Jewish Center | | qchron.com Queens
San Francisco Landmark #81: Bush Street Temple
San Francisco Landmark #118: Bnai David Temple
Congregation B'nai David and the Vanished Synagogues of San Francisco (VIRTUAL)—Jewish LearningWorks
The oldest Jewish building in Pittsburgh | The Pittsburgh Jewish Chronicle
Former Pittsburgh synagogue to become apartments, urban farm in $18.5M project | TribLIVE.com
Rauh Jewish Archives Kether Torah
Synagogue Congregation list.pdf Pittsburgh
Rauh Jewish Archives Adath Jeshurun, Pittsburgh
The Jewish Chronicle's Two-Part Series on HHCRS After It Closed | Homestead Hebrews
L'chaim on a Hilltop: Jewish Holy Houses in the Hill District (Part 2)—Pittsburgh Orbit
Monsey Memories: Sons of Jacob, "The First Synagogue in Rockland" | Rockland Daily
Temple Emanuel, Parkchester's last synagogue, closes after years of serving dwindling congregation—New York Daily News
Temple Emanuel at Parkchester: History
New Bethel Primitive Baptist/Agudath B'nai Israel Synagogue—Clio Lorain, OH
"Jewish population by city," Wikipedia
Jewish Population Estimates of Selected Cities American Jewish Year Book Information from 1950
Historic-Religious-Properties.pdf Philadelphia
hiddencityphila.org/2012/07/greater-straightaway-baptist-church-a-convoluted-architectural-voyage/ Philadelphia
Rediscovering Jewish Infrastructure: 2022 Update on United States Eighteenth and Nineteenth-Century Synagogues—American Jewish Historical Society (ajhs.org)
Historic Bayonne Synagogue Slated for Residential Redevelopment | Bayonne, NJ News TAPinto | TAPinto
Article clipped from Passaic Daily News—Newspapers.com™
1929 Dedication / Groundbreaking for Temple Emanuel in Paterson NJ | Jewish Historical Society of Northern New Jersey
The Uncertain Future of Temple Emanuel | Decopix Paterson
Brownstoner: article Building of the Day: 555 Prospect Place | Brownstoner
About Us | East Midwood Hebrew Day School
Beth-Hamedrash-Hagodol-Synagogue-370-Garden-Street.pdf CT
OUR HISTORY | Sephardic
The Forward Rabbis Want To Turn Shuttered Brooklyn Synagogue Into Halfway House—The Forward
Yeshiva Ousts 3 Black Jews as Non-Orthodox—The New York Times
MS-307: Bertha V. Corets Papers.. 1930–965.
New Zoning Law Prevents Throggs Neck Medical Office from Opening—Bronx Times
Three Torahs Stolen From Norwood Synagogue—Norwood NewsHow a Catholic school amassed a treasure trove of Jewish artifacts from the Bronx | The Times of Israel

valentine: Matt Freedman Agudas Israel Queens

When Shul Membership Was A Privilege | The Jewish Press—JewishPress.com | Israel Mizrahi

| 28 Av 5779—Thursday, August 29, 2019 | JewishPress.com Agudas Israel mentioned

Merger plans for Garden Jewish Center | | qchron.com

"We're Growing Old Together"—Garden Jewish Center in Flushing Celebrates 50 Yrs. | | qchron.com

Samuel Gruber's Jewish Art & Monuments: USA: In New Orleans, One of America's Oldest Extant Synagogue Buildings is Now Condominium Apartments

Bayside Jewish Center is closing | | qchron.com

Two Queens Synagogues Merge into Hollis Hills Bayside Jewish Center (ny1.com)

Changing demographic hurts Bayside Jewish Center—QNS

A.H. Salkowitz | Queens Modern

Three Synagogues In Queens Merge During Joyous Ceremony | | qchron.com

As Jews Move On Up To Suburbs, Temples Must Merge To Survive | | qchron.com

ArchiveGrid : Congregation Oer Chodosh Anshe Sfard Records, 1910–994 (1950s-1960s) Cleveland

Guide to the First Independent Hebrew Congregation of Jamaica (Queens, N.Y.) Records 1952–1988 (yu.edu)

Rabbi Rafael Shmuel Weiss | kevarim.com

Former Joseph Avenue synagogue will only keep its façade

Former synagogue among city properties sold at auction | News | oswegocountynewsnow.com

Yonkers' Lincoln Park Jewish Center sold to Brooklyn congregation

The History of Syracuse's Jewish Community

Kingston's Former Bridgewater Bar to become Apartments—Upstater

Steer & Turner [J.W. Steer] 1899 | Temple Emanuel—Rondout (Kingston), NY, US | Pipe Organ Database

Beth El Jacob—Friends of Albany History

History—Congregation Beth Abraham-Jacob

Samuel Gruber's Jewish Art & Monuments: Old and New Synagogues of Upstate New York:

Samuel Gruber's Jewish Art & Monuments: In a New Century Repurposed Seattle Synagogues Still Standing Tall

Hudson (samgrubersjewishartmonuments.blogspot.com)History | Congregation Anshe Emeth

Cross-river ties of faith | My Hudson Valley

SHAMOKIN: Northumberland County. | Pennsylvania PA | International Jewish Cemetery Project

In Memoriam: Former PA Jeweler Irvin R. Liachowitz | the Centurion | the Centurion

Tifereth Israel Mount Carmel

Temple Anshe Hesed—Wikipedia

## WEBSITES

### Facebook Pages:

Historical Detroit Area Architecture
Long Island Jewish History
Northeast Ohio Jewish History
Old Images of Philadelphia
Synagogues of Chicago

Suburban Jewish Community Center B'nai Aaron | Temple University ArchivesSpace Havertown
Langston Hughes Performing Arts Institute—Arts | seattle.gov
Jewish Buffalo History Center—Celebrating Jewish Buffalo Culture
JewishGen.org
Region History | International Northeast RegionInternational Northeast Region
Our History—Sinai Free Synagogue
Our History—Hebrew Institute of White Plains
Synagogues360 |
The Jewish/African-American Connection—Cleveland Restoration Society
About—Temple Shomer Emunim Toledo, OH
Heritage and History—Congregation Beth Israel CT
Welcome | tsinai (Philadelphia, Dresher)
Small Synagogues
erc/syn/queens/staten-island (museumoffamilyhistory.com)
erc/syn/brooklyn
Museum of Family History
Bronx Synagogues—Home
1940s NYC | Street photos of every building in New York City in 1939/1940
Property Taxes
Bhbi_history.pdf Rochester
NY State: ROME: (Oneida County) | New York NY | International Jewish Cemetery Project
History—Congregation Gates of Heaven (Schenectady)
New York History Review Articles: Schenectady's Jewish Immigrants: Acculturation and Preserving History
My Central New York: Tracing Syracuse's Jewish Buildings I: Former Beth Israel
History | Congregation Mishkan Or—Reform Temple in Beachwood, OH Cleveland
Our History | Har Zion Temple Philadelphia
Temple Beth Hillel-Beth El Philadelphia
Anshe Emet Synagogue—Chicago Conservative Jewish Synagogue
Our History | Emanuel Congregation | Chicago
Congregation B'nai Moshe Detroit
History Chicago Kesser Maariv
History—Temple Beth Israel Chicago/Skokie
History | Temple Beth El—Reform Temple in Bloomfield Hills, MITemple Beth El Detroit (2 sites)
rshistoryNEW.pdf CT

Congregation Agudath Sholom CT
History CT Ahavath Achim Fairfield
Reform Temple Fairfield County | Congregation B'nai Israel Bridgeport
Our History | Temple Emanuel of North Jersey Paterson
Our History—Temple B'nai Abraham Newark
History—Oheb Shalom Congregation Newark
Congregation Gates of Prayer New Orleans
History—Congregation AABJ&D Newark and suburbs
BCMH Seattle | The Orthodox Synagogue for the Entire Family—Est. 1891
Sephardic Community Center | Sephardic Synagogue | Seattle
Beth Am Israel—Soulful Shul on the Main Line—Conservative Synagogue in Philadelphia—Beth Am Israel
Home—Yeshiva of Central Queens
TAY-Our-Story.pdf
Our History & Building | Congregation Beth Emeth—Albany, NY
History—Congregation Schomre Israel
ABI Temple Lorain OH
https://www.cbitoledo.org/about-us/history-of-cbi/ Toledo, OH
www.ocfrealty.com
www.philaplace.org Philadelphia
Historic Synagogue's 22-Unit Residential Conversion Underway—Rising Real Estate
New Haverford church opens at former synagogue—Delco Times
www.isjm.org
Lost Synagogues of Detroit, Detroit
Cleveland Jewish History, Cleveland
Cleveland 's Old Still-Standing Synagogues
https://newarkreligion.com, Newark, NJ
BaltimoreJewishHistory.com

## LIBRARIES AND ARCHIVES

Jewish Theological Seminary
Yeshiva University Archives (Shulamith Berger, Head Archivist)

## MAPS

*Google Maps* has been an invaluable tool for my research.
https://www.google.com/url?q=https://chicagobikeadventures.com/former-synagogues/&sa=D&source=docs&ust=1746831595402298&usg=AOvVawoj12lzh_HJW27N6fPRlGsC
Map of Cleveland Synagogues 1850—1970—Haymarket to the Heights

## MISCELLANEOUS

Center for Jewish History (Manhattan) www.cjh.org
The Jewish Museum of New York (Manhattan) www.thejewishmuseum.org
Museum of Jewish Heritage (Manhattan) www.mjhnyc.org

www.ingramcontent.com/pod-product-compliance
Lightning Source LLC
LaVergne TN
LVHW050632100826
845148LV00011B/1837